THE BOOK OF

RESTING PLACES

THE BOOK OF
RESTING PLACES

A Personal History *of*
Where We Lay the Dead

THOMAS MIRA Y LOPEZ

COUNTERPOINT
Berkeley, California

ISBN: 978-1-61902-123-5

The Library of Congress Cataloging-in-Publication Data is available.

Jacket designed by Kelly Winton
Book designed by Wah-Ming Chang

COUNTERPOINT
2560 Ninth Street, Suite 318
Berkeley, CA 94710
www.counterpointpress.com

Printed in the United States of America
Distributed by Publishers Group West

1 3 5 7 9 10 8 6 4 2

For JTRMYL

Come down off the cross, we can use the wood.

—TOM WAITS

CONTENTS

THE BOOK OF
RESTING PLACES

MEMORY, MEMORIAL

Whenever my mother and I drive to her house in Pennsylvania, she asks me to take a look at the Ohio buckeye. It's a ritual I'm familiar with by now. I carry the bags inside and leave them on the counter, then move the food from cooler to refrigerator. She takes the black poodle out of his travel crate, praises him for being so patient, eyes him closely as he romps around the field, and when I have slid the ice packs into the freezer and the poodle has discovered for the hundredth time the hundredth smell at the base of the pine, she will call to me through the screen door. "Come, Tom, come see dad's tree."

She doesn't know how much I begrudge this ceremony. She doesn't know that, after two hours in the car next to her, all I want to do is open a bag of tortilla chips, pop the seal of a jar of salsa con queso, and stand over the counter dipping a dozen or so chips into the cheese. Or she does know this; she's my mother. If I eat too much, she knows the next thing I'll do is take a nap. She times the poodle's walk so she can call out to me before I become too involved in the process of dipping and chewing, before I feel full enough to grunt a refusal and shut the door to my room. She might even know that I do not care about the buckeye, that I attach no particular importance to it. She is my mother. She knows she has only to call my attention to it enough in order for me to care—like the way when I sit down to eat takeout with her on Monday nights, she has only to refuse to change channels and I will watch *Dancing with the Stars*.

In Pennsylvania, I trudge outside and around the house and walk up to the tree. I circle it and give the trunk a hesitant pat, squeeze its circumference, unsure of how to touch it just as I'm unsure of how to pet the dog. "It's beautiful," she'll beam, standing there, watching me. "It's grown so much."

There are five rivers in the Greek underworld: the Styx, river of hate; Acheron, river of pain; Cocytus, river of lamentation; Phlegethon, river of rage; and Lethe, river of oblivion. I like to think that, taken together, these form a rough Kübler-Ross model for ghosts. In their enumeration, Lethe comes last, the final stage of grief. Its waters serve as a general anesthetic—all those who drink from them forget their former state, their joy and grief and pleasure and pain. This potential, this river of morphine and drowsiness and opiates, sounds quite tempting when poetized, when it becomes, as Ovid writes in the *Metamorphoses*, the place "where dream-haunted poppies grow, hanging their heads above wet ferns and grasses . . . and weighted eyelids close each day to darkness."

Arriving in English from Greek via Latin, Lethe is rendered as either oblivion or forgetfulness. To me, these words mean different things: oblivion is a permanent state, forgetfulness temporary. I would like Lethe to mean the latter—a soporific that acts nightly not just to erase all memories of pain and suffering, but to restore those memories upon arising and transform them into something acceptable, a new and peaceful being. But I suspect it's really oblivion: that once you drink these waters there is no going back.

My father planted the Ohio buckeye in 2004, the year my parents bought this second house in northeastern Pennsylvania, fifteen minutes south of the Delaware River. What makes the buckeye unique is that my father planted a seed and not a sapling or nursery tree. The seed, dark brown with a café au lait spot in its center, resembles the eye of a male deer and gives the buckeye its name. By 2006, it had grown to a four-foot sapling. By 2012, my mother estimated the tree at twenty feet tall. Buckeyes grow to a height of forty-five feet. Their diameter measures fifty centimeters. They live for eighty years, a human lifespan. That is, the lifespan of a lucky human.

For my mother, it's crucial this buckeye not just live, but flourish. She'll scoff at the afterlife, yet all the same, animism and reincarnation grow within this tree. She's assigned it a spirit and wished it a narrative to fulfill these beliefs.

That spirit, of course, belongs to my father. The body is

his as well: the hands that scooped out the pocket of earth and laid the seed to rest are now the buckeye's leaves, his limbs the branches, the mind that decided to plant the tree exactly there are its roots, stretching ten feet downhill from the squat evergreen the poodle likes, thirty feet from the house so that my mother may gaze at it from the window above the kitchen sink.

One does not need to pay for passage across Lethe. Charon the toll collector ferries the dead only across the Styx or Acheron, and each must give Charon an obol, or he will not allow them to cross. An obol holds little value; it's equivalent, roughly speaking, to a worker's daily wage in Ancient Greece. If Charon does not receive his payment, the soul cannot cross and is fated to spend eternity in limbo between the world of the living and the world of the dead. To prevent this, families would place obols in the deceased's mouth, under the tongue or on the lips. This became Charon's obol: a viaticum, bus fare and a bag lunch, provision for a journey. The otherworldly narrative one can conjure from a small circular object, seed or coin, grasped in a hand.

My father's seizures began in 2003, the year before he planted the buckeye. They were minor, except when they were not, and my mother and I would spend the night next to him in a bed at Mount Sinai. Medication could treat them, except when it could not. The seizures kept recurring and, by the summer of 2006, my father, a cell biologist to whom the word *culture* meant not art but tissue cultivation, no longer worked in the garden or the field. He complained of his right hand cramping, of losing dexterity in his fingers. He no longer drank black coffee in Duralex glasses, the way he had growing up in Brazil, nor did he have a glass of Sandeman port after dinner, the way his mother had. He did not drive and this frustrated him. When I visited from college, I drove him from New York to Pennsylvania and he remained silent the whole way, watching the speedometer.

I wasn't around that summer—I worked on a farm, weeding by hand, complaining of the straw that would scratch up my arms—and so I didn't witness the regressions. I could hear them, however, if I chose to. His voice had started to slur by then, his lip a little twisted, and so he sounded over the phone as if he had just woken up from a nap, disoriented, not entirely in his present state. I wasn't around that fall either: I went to study abroad in Rome.

In September of 2006, my father suffered a massive seizure while visiting his mother in Rio de Janeiro. Two craniectomies later, the right side of his body was paralyzed and he could no longer speak. By October, he was back in New York, flown twenty-four hours in a medevac plane alongside my mother. He raised his fist in victory when they landed; he did not want to die in Brazil. She told him, when she was planning the evacuation, that he would be able to recover in the country, that they could watch the mother-of-pearl sunsets together and count sheep on the opposite hill. My father did not say anything. In November, after a little over two months of silence, he died.

∞

Unlike other memories, the buckeye does not decay or fade, but gains in strength over time. My mother can mark its progress and measure its height as if it were a growing boy. She perceives its existence as remarkable, just as she perceives mine as such—her only child, born to her at the age of forty-two, an unlikely life after a previous miscarriage. She nurtures the memory of my father before his illness—the scientist who loved trees, who loved experiments like burying seeds in the ground or sifting through bear shit he found on the road, oblivious to the implication that the bear might lurk nearby. She sees this tree and envisions a new, sturdier body, one that grows skyward without shaking or collapsing.

Despite the buckeye's heartiness, she worries. She thinks of razing the trees around it, the squat evergreen and the weeping willow, holdovers from the previous owners, even though they don't steal the buckeye's light, even though the buckeye, in fact, robs theirs. She fears she won't be able to keep it healthy, that it owes its vitality to whatever magic my father's hands held that could create a living thing.

My mother worries, in particular, because she believes herself a hopeless gardener. "Not just hopeless, I'm cursed," she'll say. I don't want to believe her (how could the woman who swaddles the poodle in a towel after his bath fail at nurturing?), but the evidence exists. The plot I weeded the year before is overgrown as ever, the sole success a transplanted peony bush. When strangers politely inquire what she grows, she snaps back, "I grow weeds." It's not immediately clear that

she's serious. Rumors of her inadequacy apparently spread. The
gardener who lives down the road does not return her calls and
she does not know why. "I'm cursed, I'm doomed," she'll say.
She has left several messages, asking for his services, offering
him to name his price, but he has not called back.

To keep the tree alive, she's enlisted my help. I weed the
base of the buckeye, lay down mulch and wood chips. I build
a wire fence around its perimeter to keep out rabbits. We both
have no idea what we're doing, but these acts are of utmost importance—if I refuse or complain, the tree's life hangs in the
balance, we could lose my father all over again—and so we walk
out and admire it each visit, as if we were visiting a living tomb,
as if we were trying to grow the thing on good karma alone.

In 2008, as the buckeye made its ascent, my mother bought a
tree in Central Park in memory of my father. A horse chestnut,
specifically. It stands in the North Meadow, along the path my
father walked each morning to and from work. Standing beside this tree, you can see Mount Sinai to the east. The hospital's medical center, a large black building, fills the skyline. My
father worked in this building and was transferred there as a
patient after my mother flew him out of Brazil. This was where
he died. Adjacent to the horse chestnut lie the fields where he
watched me play soccer growing up—I was the goalkeeper,
he the assistant coach by virtue of being Brazilian. Nearby, a
five-minute walk away, are the trees where he buried the pet
hamster and cockatiel on his way to work, after we found them
at the bottom of their cages.

∞

The New York Times is profiling the dangers of the city's trees. Like my father, Elmaz Qyra liked to walk in the park after work. When he had finished his shift as a busboy, he walked a few blocks north to the 59th Street entrance and headed to Poet's Walk. One time in late February 2010, he went for a walk after a heavy snow had fallen. At 3:00 p.m., the *Times* wrote, if there was any sunlight, Poet's Walk must have been wondrous. The park, Qyra's wife said, reminded him of the farm where he grew up in Albania. What Qyra did not know, as he walked alone along the promenade, was that one of the trees above him was due to be removed. The year before, a limb had fallen from it and damaged another tree. A five-foot cavity swelled within its trunk. A fatal fungus infested it. When Elmaz Qyra passed beneath the tree, a fifteen-foot limb as heavy as a refrigerator fell, split his head open, and killed him.

After my father was hospitalized in Rio, I visited him there. I flew from Rome and stayed for two weeks. My mother was already there. Over those two weeks, my father in and then out of the ICU, I gained ten pounds. I liked the food in the hospital cafeteria and it killed time. There wasn't much to do: hold my father's hand, read Graham Greene, watch soccer or CNN, masturbate in the shower, nap, wipe the sweat from my father's forehead, play solitaire on my iPod. Staying overnight in the hospital room, I would sleep from eight in the evening till ten the next morning. I told my mother on a taxicab ride back to my grandmother's that I wanted to go back to Rome. I told her I was upset I was missing out on life. She asked me whether I wanted to be part of a family or not. She lost fifteen pounds and started smoking again, exhaling a lot, smoke or sighs. She sighed so audibly and so out of the blue that I thought she did so on purpose, to catch my attention or await my comment, but she said she didn't even know she was doing it.

My father lost even more weight, nearly thirty pounds if I had to guess. Half a pound came from his skull. A human skull weighs a little over two pounds, and doctors removed a quarter of my father's to perform their second craniectomy. They did not install a plate and so the left side of my father's head looked deflated. There seemed nothing separating brain from skin. The scalp, hair shaved to a stubble, flapped and breathed of its own accord. If I pressed hard enough with my finger, I thought I would touch brain.

My father didn't have much of an appetite. I began to eat the soft, warm foods off his tray: macaroni and cheese, applesauce, mashed potatoes, flan. The nurses who brought in the meals would do a song and dance each time about how delicious the food looked, how hungry my father must be, how he needed sustenance to get his strength back up. I looked on while they did this, picking out which food I would eat first, the nurses not knowing they were performing for me.

To eat and sleep, of course, is its own form of forgetting. If you were not awake for it, it's hard to say it really happened.

∞

I cannot see the buckeye the way my mother sees it. My father does not stand tall within it, this ugly thing choking the water and stealing sunlight away from the evergreen. Its growth is not representative of his spirit. There are few memories for me of my father in the country, none of his working the land. When my parents first bought this house, during the visit when my father planted this seed, I stayed in New York. I was still in high school and their overnight trips meant that I could have friends over and hotbox the bathroom.

Still, I yearn to see it with my mother's eyes. Now he rises balanced, where before there was asymmetry and paralysis. Now he grows and feeds on water, where before he shrank, withered from the inability to retain fluid. Now bark armors the pith within his trunk, where before nothing encased his cerebral tissue or separated it from his skin. The wind rustles through his leaves and sometimes it even howls, where before there was only silence.

This is all, I suspect, just another way of forgetting. Or of remembering only what we want to remember. The river of Lethe runs underground and feeds the buckeye. By placing my father in this tree, my mother chooses to remember him as she prefers: as strong and healthy, flourishing instead of decaying. I do not fault her for that—it dulls the pain.

Form, however, collapses. My father's body, my mother's superstitions. And what happens when the surface can no longer hide the structural frailty underneath? Trees rot, desiccate, become infested, drink too deeply from poisonous waters. Oblivion lasts until a branch snaps and falls with the anger of being forgotten.

∞

Within her own memory, my mother has begun to mix up names. She calls me Rafael for my father. She calls the dog Tom. She calls my father Tom or Celso, the poodle's name. Sometimes she says *your dad*, when she means *your grandfather.* What's more, she no longer catches the slip. I used to correct her every time, jumping on the chance of being right. Now I let it slide.

"Do you visit dad's tree?" she'll ask, meaning the horse chestnut she purchased in Central Park. I tell her not so much. I rarely have reason to pass it—I no longer play soccer or baseball on those fields; I have no desire to cross the park and visit Mount Sinai. I read a book underneath it once, Salinger's *Nine Stories.* "No, Mom," I'll say, "I was a mile away." I ask her if she ever visits and she says she doesn't often end up around there, it's out of her way and hard to reach. She means that from there she can see that big black building in the east. But she's glad the tree's there all the same.

In the *Times,* I learn of more cases like Elmaz Qyra's—dozens of incidents over the past decade, resulting in at least ten lawsuits against the city. In 2009, the year before Qyra died, a thirty-three-year-old Google engineer, father of two, was struck by a hundred-pound branch from an oak thirty-seven feet above him. He suffered traumatic brain injuries, paralysis, and damage to his spinal cord and lungs; his lawsuit, still pending, is worth $120 million. In June of 2010, a branch fell on a mother and her six-month-old daughter outside the Central Park Zoo, killing the infant. What seemed highly improbable—a fate for those with bad karma, for the superstitious to fear—has now entered the realm of possibility. The realm where we should be more careful about what hangs over our heads.

Adrian Benepe, then New York City Parks commissioner, made a statement that the only way to prevent falling branches would be to cut down all of the city's trees, a measure that would do more harm than good. The Central Park Conservancy writes: "The trees of Central Park have an important impact on the urban environment. They improve the quality of our air and water; reduce storm water runoff, flooding, and erosion; and lower the air temperature in the summer. This is why Central Park is called the lungs of New York City." Benepe further added after Qyra's accident, "There is no reason to believe anything else might happen like that."

At my grandparents' house growing up, my cousins and I would play a game called Monster under my grandfather's horse chestnut tree. The horse chestnut was so large one did not near it but enter it, a 200-year-old cathedral of a tree whose limbs ran down along the ground for thirty feet before rising up one hundred. My father would chase us around the yard, his face twisted into a rictus, lip upturned into sneer. "Now I'm coming to get you," he would shout, once he had given us enough time to reach safety. If my father found and caught us, he would wrap us up in his arms and the game would be over. To avoid him, we hid under the canopy of the horse chestnut tree. When we heard him coming, his stomp and growl, we began to climb. We climbed a limb near the tree's edge, one that ran along the ground until it rose upward again. My father would palm open the curtain of leaves and scowl, feigning disorientation, giving us time, pretending he did not know we had run to where we always ran. For reasons unexplained, he could not climb the tree, so elevation proved our safe haven. If we climbed beyond his grasp and kicked free of the hands that grabbed our ankles, he could do nothing but look up at us—our chests swelling against the bark, feet dangling—and glower. Then the game would end.

Eventually a branch necessary to climb this limb snapped off. It was our first foothold and, without it, we were helpless. My father nailed a two-by-four to the trunk where the branch had been. Our feet could not wrap around it the same way, but it remained fixed and we could climb the limb again. I know that even if this limb were to continue growing, this two-by-four would stay in the same place and persist, at the perfect height for a four-year-old's step. This plank, to me, is stable memory, oblivion's antithesis. That is, until a new owner decides to prune the branches, or lightning strikes the thing, or Hurricane Sandy or Amelia or Rachel or Alexandra or Hannah moves in off the Atlantic, or the branch just rots and poisons the tree and I die.

The last time I heard my father speak was on my birthday. I was in the shower, in Rome, and my cell phone rang. I turned off the water and answered. It was October and my mother was at Mount Sinai. She wished me happy birthday and put him on the phone. He was doing better and could form a few sounds. Mostly sighs. The word *hey*. He made it halfway through *happy birthday*. I waited on the other end, head leaning against the tiles, naked, dripping wet.

The last time I heard him speak a complete sentence was at the airport in late August before I flew to Rome from New York. I had an evening flight, and he was to fly to Rio de Janeiro the following day. I don't remember what he said, not knowing what the moment meant. But it must have been along the lines of: "Be safe, Tom. Remember x, remember y. Love you. Be safe."

I asked my mother why they didn't call me from the hospital more often, if my father could manage a few words. She said she didn't really know. "Dad was tired," she said, "It was very hard for him. He preferred silence." Now it's hard to know how he felt about us, if he was mad I wasn't there, if I was acting the right way or hurting him further. We could have just remained speechless over the line, but I do not say that, just as my mother does not ask me why I did not call the hospital myself, why I stayed in Rome.

The above is not exactly true. The last time I heard my father's voice was a few years after his death. He had recorded the message on the answering machine at the house in Pennsylvania. I would call from time to time, when I knew my mother was not there. His voice sounded distracted, caught off guard, because either my mother or I had just walked into the room. You could hear the kitchen chair creak as he leaned in to begin recording.

I didn't tell my mother I would listen, but I am almost certain she did the same because sometime later, when I was away or abroad, she changed the recording to an automated message and erased his last remaining words. Though I wouldn't have done so, I only hope the agony of deleting his voice, the willful choice to try and forget it, weighed less for her than the pain of its reminder.

While there's no account of what Elmaz Qyra heard before he died, others describe the sound of a falling branch in various ways. A thunderclap. Or the creak of a floorboard in a horror movie. A booming. A loud crack or snap. It sounds like something. A warning or a taunt or a condemnation.

Trees rot because of fungus and internal decay. A tree suffers a significant wound, anything larger than three to four inches in diameter, and fungi will establish their presence in the time it takes it to form a callous over the injury. It's a common phenomenon for a tree to suffer significant injury: lightning can strike or a thunderstorm can break a limb; roots can be damaged underground or insects can infest it; there's human harm, say someone who prunes one large limb instead of several smaller ones. As a defense mechanism, trees will compartmentalize their decay to maintain structural integrity. That is, fungi will only rot away the dead wood in the center of the tree. A tree can sustain the hollowing of its core as long as new rings are forming and widening around its circumference; its structure can bear a central emptiness if there is something to compensate. Just like humans do, I figure. Some trees do a better job of compartmentalizing decay than others. Oaks, for example. Some trees do not. Hackberries. Ash. Horse chestnuts.

Technically, my mother did not buy the horse chestnut tree in Central Park, but an endowment for it. The Tree Trust of the Central Park Conservancy offers New Yorkers the opportunity to "create a living memory that will last for generations to come." In exchange for a donation, the Conservancy will engrave a paving stone along the southern end of Poet's Walk. The endower receives the more or less false sense that he or she owns a tree.

Donations range depending on the tree endowed. For $1,000, you can purchase a new sapling. For $5,000, "a remarkable tree" and an engraved granite paving stone. For $12,000, a tree cluster family. For $25,000, a historic tree, planted 150 years ago at Central Park's inception. For $250,000, you can purchase allées. Allées are "a unique arrangement of two or more rows of the same species." The example the Conservancy gives is of the majestic American elms along Poet's Walk itself. With these come an engraved bronze plaque.

My mother purchased a remarkable tree. Her engraved granite paving stone reads somewhere on Poet's Walk: *Endowed by JUDY THOMAS in honor of RAFAEL MIRA Y LOPEZ*. But I am not sure. I've never visited.

∞

I flew from Rome to New York in early November. I landed on a Thursday and was scheduled to fly back on Sunday, but my father died that Sunday night and so I stayed. That day, around noon or one in the afternoon, a doctor told my mother and me that my father would not last very long. I told my mother I would be right back. I took the elevator down the eight or nine floors from the ICU my father had been moved into the night before and stepped out onto the street. Across Fifth Avenue was Central Park and I began to run. I ran into the park, past the dust field, past the North Meadow, past the horse chestnut, out onto the Upper West Side and north ten blocks until I reached the Cathedral of St. John the Divine. I entered and told the man behind the donation booth that I would like to buy the $3.95 candle. I handed him a twenty and he told me he could not make change and pointed to a sign. I left, bought an apricot Linzer cookie at the pastry shop next door, came back, put a five-dollar bill on the counter, took my candle, and threw the cookie at the man. I walked down the nave until I reached the bed of candles by the altar. I laid the wick in a neighboring candle's flame and placed mine among the others. Written on the glass of the other candles were messages and well-wishes for loved and lost ones. I did not write anything, but I did make a wish. A wish that, if I were to say what it was, I'd be afraid wouldn't come true.

I took a cab back to the hospital. I watched the New York Giants lose to the Chicago Bears, and that night, figuring things would hold, I told my mother I was going back to the apartment. I'd have a bite to eat and get some rest. My aunt had just driven down and we ordered take-out, General Tso's chicken and scallion pancakes. The food arrived and a call came from my mother. "You should come back," she said. I did. When I arrived, my father seemed the same and I fell asleep in an armchair at the foot of the bed. The overnight nurse came and left and, after she did so, when his breathing began to shallow, my mother told me, "You should come to the bed, Tom."

A *remarkable tree* is an interesting name for a common horse chestnut, especially when one considers that the Conservancy is naming things that do not know they have names. But a re-markable tree is exactly what my mother believes this chestnut to be.

Endowments help ensure the maintenance of Central Park, but the Conservancy does not inform you what happens if your particular tree is damaged or destroyed. This is a valid concern. On Halloween in 2011, an unprecedented snowstorm damaged one thousand trees in Central Park. Earlier that year, Hurricane Irene destroyed one hundred trees.

Before these, a thunderstorm downed more than one hun-dred trees in the park on August 19, 2009. Hundreds more were damaged, many fatally. This was the most severe destruc-tion the park's trees had sustained in decades, and it was con-centrated in the northern third of the park, where my father's horse chestnut stood. The storm was a microburst: straight-line winds reached speeds of seventy miles per hour. "Central Park has been devastated," said Adrian Benepe. "You have personal relationships with certain trees and now they are gone." "We're not going to be around in eighty years when they grow back," said Donna Castellano, director of operations of the cardiology department in the big black building at Mount Sinai.

The storm lasted from around 10:00 to 10:30 p.m., a time when five years earlier my father would have been walking home from work, when I would have been in another part of the park, getting high with my friends. The storm destroyed another horse chestnut close to my father's, near the entrance at 100th Street. The city temporarily closed the fields at North Meadow because of safety concerns.

My father's chestnut went unscathed. "It was terrible," my mother reported to me, "but what a miracle. Nothing happened to dad's tree. It was so lucky." The tree survived with only a few broken branches. It had earned its remarkableness.

After you watch someone die, an odd minute passes when you are unsure what to do next. It's a minute removed from time's flow, even though you are very sure of what time it is. When my father died, this happened. The nurses were not yet informed, the hall was silent, it was 11:11 p.m. There was not much for us to do. I did not know whether I was allowed or supposed to touch him. What I did—with the knowledge that one day I would look back, hovering over myself to scrutinize these actions—was take a penny from my pocket and place it in my father's hand. This was not easy. I had to uncurl his hand (his right hand, the one that had been paralyzed, though now it made no difference), stick the penny against the palm's flesh, and then close the hand again. But the penny would not stay put, his hand did not want to close, and so I wedged it in between his index and middle fingers, near the lowest knuckle.

Why I did this puzzles me. It wasn't Charon's obol exactly—I did not open my father's mouth and lay the coin on his tongue—but it was an act of superstition. I'm not a pagan or a polytheist; I don't believe in Hades or the underworld. I am the son of a scientist. But, all the same, I told my mother as I struggled with his hand, "He might need this."

I believe now that this was not just superstition, but forgetting. Passage paid not for Acheron or Styx, but for Lethe. I was, in a way, trying to obscure memory, to make surreal or unreal what I would otherwise have to account for as the truth. I was not being me, but watching myself be me. That bad old habit of pretending you're a character in a movie: this is one way of dealing with a situation you are unprepared for, to watch what motions you will go through as if from a distance. I watched myself put a penny in my father's hand because I knew I would later replay that moment and not what happened the minute before. I ran a mile and a half to the cathedral when I could have taken a cab because to run was more cinematic.

Milton calls Lethe the "wat'ry labyrinth, whereof who drinks, forthwith his former state and being forgets." I say Lethe because, when I look back, I see someone other than myself going through those motions. I see someone who, when not eating or sleeping, was wrapped up in the business of being another; who already then was planting a seed to obscure the past; who was busy constructing a labyrinth of oblivion. I see a boy who was prepared to wave happily goodbye to memory and his father if it meant circumnavigating the rivers of hate, pain, lamentation, and rage. I see someone content to lose sight, to let the boat slip into slick, still fog, if all it left him was a penny poorer.

The trees Elmaz Qyra walked underneath were the allées, the American elms of Poet's Walk, purchasable for $250,000. "These elms," the Conservancy writes, "are one of the largest and last remaining stands in North America, and one of the Park's most photographed areas." It goes on: "They form a cathedral-like canopy above the Park's widest pedestrian pathway." The American elm that killed Qyra, the one scheduled to be removed, the one within which a five-foot cavity swelled, was given a special name for the way it always appeared bathed in light. It was called the Ghost Elm.

I called my mother to find out what she inscribed along Poet's Walk and discovered I had it wrong. She said she did not buy an endowment for a horse chestnut. She wanted to but they had none available. She had bought an endowment for an American elm.

Midway through *The Aeneid*, Aeneas descends to the underworld and reunites with his father Anchises. When the Greeks sacked Troy, Aeneas fled the city carrying his elderly father upon his back. Before he reaches what will become Rome, before Dido and Carthage, Aeneas lands at the city of Drepanum in Sicily. There, Anchises dies. A year or so later, Aeneas breaks off a golden bough, gives it as a gift to Proserpina, Pluto's queen, and wins entrance into the underworld. When eventually he finds his father there, he sees a multitude of people drinking from a river and asks Anchises what they are doing. Anchises tells him: "They are the souls who are destined for Reincarnation; and now at Lethe's stream they are drinking the waters that quench man's troubles, the deep draught of oblivion . . . They come in crowds to the river Lethe, so that, you see, with memory washed out they may revisit the earth above."

So, you see, I had it backwards. The living do not drink from Lethe; the dead do. It is not my mother and I who drink for oblivion, but my father. Its waters wash his subterranean roots, wipe out all memories of pain and agony and paralysis and monstrosity, and perhaps, I hope, restore him to balance and peace. A tree that readies itself to grow and survive, to stand in symmetry, to speak in whispers and wind but to speak nonetheless. He would, of course, in his preparation for earthly life, forget all else. He would forget us, his wife and child; he would have to. It's a fair trade, I think. The most my mother and I could hope for is something animate, something spirited and numinous to pass between us, some flash of sun to glance off the buckeye and catch my mother's eye at the kitchen window, or some pattern of light and shade to fall across the pages of my book as I sit on a rock underneath my father the Remarkable American Elm.

Let us pause on that rock, that tree, that American elm that survived one thunderstorm and the others to come. Let us stage another cinematic scene. Imagine an incision of three to four inches in diameter, imagine a fungus creeping in, imagine decay and rot and the loss of integrity. Imagine the penny was needed, but it fell loose from his hand. Imagine that Lethe was the wrong river all along, that really we are still stuck on the Styx or Acheron or Cocytus or Phlegethon, that the waters still bubble with hate and pain and lamentation and rage. Imagine there is no end, no true forgetting, that whatever already happened will continue to gnaw and plague and eat away at me and my father and mother. Imagine that's how eternity works. And now imagine I have actually come to visit my father's tree, to sit on the rock underneath its branches and read a book and occasionally look out at the children playing soccer and, farther away, the large black building where he died. And imagine what if, just what if, the sound I heard before the branch fell and split open a quarter of my skull was not a boom or crack or thunder or creak but a voice, his deprived voice, and it was mad as all hell and it said to me, "You motherfucker, you monster, you tried to sleep and eat your way past me, you tried to pretend I wasn't there, you piece of shit, you stayed away while I was dying, you ingrate, you fuck, you ordered Chinese food two hours before my death, you asshole, you were content to let me go if it made your life easier, you selfish son of a bitch. But now I'm coming to get you."

MONUMENT VALLEY

With the invention of the daguerreotype in the mid-nineteenth century, Americans adopted a strange tradition. They took family photographs of their dead.

Families dressed the bodies of children or parents in their finest clothes, then sat them in a rocking chair or laid them out on a divan. Sometimes, they stood the body up and relatives gathered around the corpse, Christmas card–like. Often, given the rates of infant mortality and the relative novelty of the medium, this was the only family photo that existed.

It's a morbid habit, but not a new one. Pliny writes famously that painting "originated in tracing lines round the human shadow," just as early daguerreotype advertisements claimed the technology would "catch the substance ere the shadow fades." Right at the onset of a new technology, one whose future iterations would so display the muscles and ripples of movement—of what it means to be alive—people used it to do what they've always done: capture their dead.

For many years I owned a flip phone. When I finally bought an iPhone, I downloaded a game. This was a big step for me; I'm not an iPhone sort of guy. But *Monument Valley*, its creators promised, was a game full of "illusory adventure, impossible architecture, and forgiveness." That sounded good. Ida, a young girl in a white dress and conical hat, navigates different levels, each with its own fantastic structure: ruins of cities, mazes, a jeweler's box of mirrored rooms, waterfalls falling out of empty buildings.

The game plays with perspective. Ida begins a level at one spot and through a reshuffling of architectural and geographical elements, she M. C. Eschers herself to a point far distant. For much of the game, you manipulate angles, tapping and swiping until the physically impossible occurs. Columns appear different sizes or a stairway seems to end in midair, but then the structure is twisted round and a path beckons toward a place previously inaccessible.

Sometimes, crows pester the landscape, blocking Ida's path, cawing at her with their big, loud beaks. A holographic figure called the Ghost, the game's storyteller and cliché old wise man, floats around and offers equal parts wisdom and scolding. Mostly, though, *Monument Valley* is a solitary game. You and Ida figure a problem out. I played in bed in the morning or before I turned out the lights at night. When Ida reaches the end of a level, she takes off her hat and sets loose a spinning geometric shape. It floats in the air and lands on an altar. This is her offering, her ritual, her monument. The game hinges on its mystery: What does she offer and whom does she offer it to? What does she seek "forgiveness" for?

Something uncanny happens in these photographs of the dead. Daguerreotype exposures took notoriously long to develop, and living subjects needed to sit still for prolonged stretches, minutes sometimes with their heads braced and bodies propped perfectly still. Often, since the dead died at all ages and the family dressed identically and assumed monochromatically placid expressions, it becomes difficult to determine, when looking at a photo, just who is the corpse. It's only when you study two pairs of hands under their cuffs—one a shade darker than the other—or notice how one family member sags a bit against a cushion, that you find the detail that separates living from dead.

These photos must have confused a sense of order. We say the living and the dead should not mix. The dead live in the land of the unknown and, if someone shuffles that seemingly impossible path back to the living, then something has gone wrong. Orpheus and Eurydice. The night watchman and the ringing of the corpse's bell. A ghost is a manifestation of guilt, a forgiveness demanded, a memory contested. Our way of dealing with the uncomfortable truth: the dead do not return to life, but they do return to the living.

Like a daguerreotype, an iPhone is an intimate object. You hold one in your hand. You cradle it sometimes. There, relatively cheap and available, hovers the past.

About three-quarters of the way through *Monument Valley* comes the twist. The Ghost upbraids Ida—"Shameful Ida, why do you come back here?"—and she lowers her head. When she does, we realize her hat forms an inverted beak and that she and the crows are one and the same. Like the game's architecture, we have only witnessed her from one perspective. Ida is in mourning, and each sacred shape she returns is also one she stole. Her monuments disguise her thefts, her paths through these ruins her penance.

Once I stood in a cherry orchard on a hill overlooking Prague. I had just turned twenty and, although I did not know it, my father was about to die. It was Halloween and I would dress up that night as one of the seven deadly sins. I seemed to be both myself and not myself at the same time.

The cherry orchard still had its leaves. They were yellow and magnificent and carpeted the ground. There were rows and rows of cherry trees, so many that wherever I stopped there were four directions to choose from. It seemed these paths were multiplying, that they formed all possible paths one could take in a life.

When I stopped walking the orchard, I climbed a tree. The fruit still hung from the branches and I ate too many cherries and spat the pits out on the ground. Sitting up in that tree, I wondered: When are you most yourself? Is it when you do what you do every day, or is it when you do something for the first time? Like say when you dress up as Greed for Halloween—are you more yourself then or less yourself? Like say when you find out someone you love will die. Are you more yourself or less yourself? Like say when you're gone and someone tries to capture your ghost.

I climbed down from the tree. I wiped my jeans off and picked one last cherry from the ground. I walked back along the same path. The rows and rows of cherry trees merged and it no longer felt as if I could walk down all possible paths, as if they held all potential sums and endings. I figured it didn't matter one way or the other.

For a long time after that, I thought memory worked like an encyclopedia. In order to remember someone, I would need all our experiences alphabetized and annotated. I must not forget anything.

Then I thought, since the person I knew was only one aspect of the person who lived, I'd also need the memories of all the people close to him. We'd layer them one around the other, like a tree with its rings, so that the form of the whole was dependent upon the advancement of each part.

But if I needed all the memories of those who knew this man, I'd also need the memories of those who didn't: the woman who brushed his hand on a subway pole, the stranger who didn't talk to him on a plane. The flower bed he weeded, the family pet, his favorite tree—I would need to give these language and add them to the book as well.

Yet even this wasn't enough. Because what I really needed was the experience of the person himself, the person lost. And for this, he would have needed to have kept his own encyclopedic account. Still, this record would only exist of that one person at one specific time, and so unless he recorded every single thing that happened at every single moment (every passing thought, every urge, every decision or indecision he did or did not make), the book would be incomplete. And if he did record everything that happened, he would do this and only this for all of his life and thus have no real life to live.

I didn't know what to do. I grew angry for a long time. And, of course, the person I most wanted to talk to about this was the very person I was trying to remember.

Though I did not know it, I was thinking of Monument Valley. The place, I mean. When viewers first saw its footage in John Ford's *Stagecoach* in 1939, they made the mistake of assuming this site, one of the most photographed on earth, stood in for all of the American West. The land of the unknown—its myth, its grandeur, its memory—rendered in five square cinemascope miles.

If all that unknown land is out there, I thought, how do we choose just one path to stand in for all the rest? What is the right memory in the face of all we'll forget? I began to suspect that the mind that haunts its past is not the shadow but its captor. That a ghost—the being that seeks forgiveness, the being that returns when something has gone wrong—isn't necessarily the one who's dead.

A PLAN FOR THE AFTERLIFE

My mother announces that when she dies, she wants to be buried like the pharaohs. We talk over the phone and I imagine her sitting in what used to be my father's green chair, surveying the frames and cabinets that crowd the walls, feet bouncing on the footstool, the black poodle perched alertly on her lap. I ask her why and she cackles back: "Because they get to take all their stuff with them!" She means, of course, that the ruling classes of Ancient Egypt buried themselves alongside their most prized possessions, rooms full of them sometimes, because these objects brought them pleasure and sustenance in the afterlife. My mother neither likes nor believes in immortality, yet she certainly doesn't mind the idea of always remaining with the things she loves, the things that could fill a room. Or a storage unit. With a location on 135th Street and Riverside Drive, Manhattan Mini Storage is only a mile away from her apartment and "it would be a piece of cake," she tells me, to move her cremains and other belongings into an eight-by-ten foot, climate-controlled cube. I wouldn't even have to hire movers.

My mother says many things about her afterlife. At seventy-three, she's at an age when long-standing intractability rubs up against a mind grown mercurial. First, she asks for her ashes to be laid alongside her parents' within the low stone wall out back of the Episcopalian church in East Hampton. Next she tells me I'm to drop hers and my father's ashes into the lake in the Adirondacks where we used to spend summers. "Which one?" I ask, since we stayed at two, Abanakee and Indian. "Oh, Indian Lake, of course," she scoffs. "Abanakee is man-made!" Now her plan is for me to bury hers, my father's, and the poodle's ashes in the field next to her country house in Pennsylvania. "And where will I go?" I ask. "You don't want to be with us in the country?" "Not really," I say. "Well then, it looks like you're out of luck!" And she laughs, the poodle yapping along in accompaniment, until the laugh sounds something like a roar, grown more and more phlegmy as she ages so that now it resembles one of her sister's hoary outbursts. It's a way, on some level, of masking the fact she'd rather not be laughing at all.

The Ancient Egyptians lavished such attention on death you could say that they lived to die. Death held such importance because it wasn't exactly death; instead, the Egyptians saw it as a period of limbo and the afterworld a perilous journey, filled with spitting serpents and fiery lakes, four-horned bulls and monkeys that cut the heads off unwary travelers. At the journey's end, the dead weighed their hearts against a feather. If the heart proved lighter, then the dead were reborn in another realm. If the heart proved heavier, a monster with the head of a crocodile, the torso of a lion, and the hindquarters of a hippopotamus devoured the heart's owner. All in all, a daunting schlep.

The most important event in a person's life was to build one's tomb. Wealthy Egyptians commissioned mastabas, monoliths built some thirty feet high from the mud of the Nile, sloping upward like a pyramid sliced off at its base. A mastaba, with its cache of false doors and hidden statues, served as a monumental storage unit: its burial chamber lay hidden underground, the tunnel down to it rocked up with rubble so that the body and its possessions—what was most vulnerable, most inviolable—stayed secret and safe.

For a quarter century, my mother's welcome mat has read *Go Away*. A joke, I'd explain to visitors, although was it really? Human contact brings pain. Ask about her childhood and she'll say that the boys in third grade threw rocks at her. Ask her to search further back and she'll speculate that when she was four, driving down a country road outside Baltimore, her sister Abby pushed her out of the car, her parents blithely motoring on until several minutes later a gleeful refrain emanated from the back: "Judy fell out of the car, Judy fell out of the car,

Judy fell out of the car!" My mother lay in the median, head cracked open and bleeding, an injury she says still gives her headaches today. After my father died and I later moved across the country to Arizona, my mother was left on her own, save for the dog, in an apartment full of things once shared. There she found herself underground, sealed off from what was once most valuable.

Now she must adapt. A few years ago, she capitulated and bought a cell phone, though she often leaves it turned off. "Nobody calls me anyway, I never have any voicemails," she says, the reason being that she doesn't know how to check her voicemail. If I call her cell from the other side of the country, always my last resort, she answers only after five or six rings. As often as not, she's taken the dog to the groomer and I can picture her fumbling with the thing, holding it up as if it were an alien object, fearful of what might pop out when she flips it open, the poodle puzzled and patient at her feet. Upon answering, she will clear her throat and say, "Hello?" and then, immediately again, much louder this time, "Hello!!!" as if she were trying to greet the satellite itself. And then I hear "What the fuck is wrong with this?" and she will hang up without waiting for an answer, unaware her voice has been drowning out mine the entire time.

Besides the obvious complications, my mother's plan poses some problems. Take grave robbers, for example.

Most Egyptologists deem it rare to uncover a tomb, even a small one, that's not been repeatedly looted. The men who robbed mastabas were often the ones who built them: thieves came armed with the exact location of underground chambers, tunneling down to a point beneath the room's ceiling, before breaking through a side wall, gathering the dead's possessions, and tunneling back out. Sometimes a corpse is found, the bones crushed where the underground walls collapsed, the thief turned to artifact himself, left to survive the afterlife with only the possessions stolen from another.

Aware of this, my mother has taken precautions. She's flagged suspected looters and decreed that under no circumstances are family members—specifically, her sisters and nieces—allowed into her apartment after her death. "They're snoops, they'll poke around, they'll steal all my treasures," she says. "Surely," I tell her, "you can't be serious." After she dies, I'm to bar the doors, opening them only for appraisers from Doyle Gallery. Pharaohs sometimes buried themselves alongside their pets and servants and so I ask her, "What about me?"—the only son returning to find he's shuttered inside the dead widow's two-bedroom apartment, riding out the siege amidst the clutter and leftover dog, the past lives slipped into the fabric and framework of the five rooms and one hall. Leave it to my mother to devise the most antisocial wake imaginable. But she, hearing a different question, brushes it aside: "No, Tom, I'm not worried about you taking anything. You've no eye for good stuff!"

This eye matters. The Egyptians believed the spirit divided into three parts—the *ka*, *ba*, and *akh*—and each required care to survive the afterlife. The *ka*, the dead body's physical double, demanded all sustenance necessary during life: food and drink to give it energy, possessions for comfort and entertainment, attention and care from those keeping vigil. If looters and grave robbers stole from the dead, they stole what kept the dead alive.

This forms the kernel of my mother's wish: that materiality not lose its practicality, even in death. Or maybe it's my own unvoiced hope—nothing will disappear but merely transition. There is no end, only a false door to pass back and forth through. If I just preserve her in the right way, if I go down to the CVS and buy the proper embalming fluid and select the correctly sized canopic jars, then I prepare the way for her to last as long as the garnets and opals, the rose quartz and uncut amethyst she so lovingly collects.

Yet what happens if nobody is there to bar the door?

After my grandmother moved from East Hampton to a retirement home in Manhattan, my family packed up her house. My aunts and nieces arrived first and, in my mother's words, "took all the best stuff"—the letters my grandmother kept, her finest set of sterling silverware, her books on Chartres. My mother has been tracking these down ever since, thinking that if she recovers her mother's prized possessions, she'll recover her mother herself.

It also gives her the chance to snoop. The other year at my cousin Ralph's apartment in Vermont, she opened his closet door while looking for the bathroom. There she found, sitting on a shelf, a statue of a bull, its body twisted, horns torqued, iron rusting over like lichen. "This is where it's been!" she cried out, loud enough that the rest of the family put down their chopsticks and looked up from their pad Thai. She emerged victorious from the closet, her eyes aglow, bull raised in front of her like a sacrificial victim. "I've been looking for this for years! You had it hiding in there the whole time. I just love this bull!"

This was not enough. The mystery—how it traveled from my grandmother's in East Hampton to a dark shelf in Montpelier—required solution. "Who gave this to you?" She stationed herself between Ralph and the table where his mother and three daughters ate. "My mother did, I suppose," he said. "And where did she get it?" She put her hands on her hips in mock seriousness.

His mother, my aunt Abby, called across the table. "Oh that was years ago, Judy, who can remember?" My mother ignored this, believing Abby the thief, and turned back to Ralph. "Well you can't really want it if it's just sitting in your closet gathering dust?" Ralph shrugged and, just like that, my mother pocketed the bull.

Now it sits by her living room window, weighing down the record player I gave her for Christmas. This is not theft to her, but an act of reclamation, something her own mother would have wanted. "She knew I appreciated these things more. They just don't have an eye for them," she says of her sisters as she says of me. "Did you see that awful rug Abby spent $500 on? It looks like a python regurgitated its prey!"

When my mother finds an object she loves, she will say she's bonded with it. It's an attachment—to bond is to be bound—but it's also something more. A bond is a covalence. Electrons shared, atoms stabilized, the life of one body tied to another. Possessions become both vocation and evocation. If her house is to be looted, she'll at least have the satisfaction of knowing how impressed everyone will be with her accumulations and arrangements, how at-home that print of her mother-in-law looks hung on the wall or how the iron bull on the record player catches the afternoon light. Her objects retain an objectivity; she displays them and they display her. She remains, as she likes to call herself, a *picker*, a salvager of the neglected and underappreciated.

This is the fate of the old widowed woman: to fade into the room she's spent her life arranging.

The *ba*, the second part of the soul, was an avian sphinx, a bird with a human head. It rose from its burial chamber each morning to fly through the mastaba's false doors and sun itself in the open air. The Egyptians believed birds' chirping to be the conversations of *bas*, gossiping and flitting their day away in idle chitchat like two old friends over the telephone.

When days or weeks slip by and I feel guilty for not having called her and it remains a mystery what she does with all her time in the house alone, no company save the over-vigilant poodle, my mother will tell me the next time we talk that she feels invisible. She forms these words slowly, as if a child puzzling over a new sentence. "I feel like I could just float off into the air and nobody would notice," she says. Now, to fill her time, she holds conversations with the dead. She tells me she summons her parents into the room. I ask how she does it and she says, "I just open the door and invite them inside for a cup of tea." Then, after a pause, she adds: "I ran into something I wrote a while ago. It was called, 'I Only Talk to the Dead and Animals.' Wouldn't that be a good name for a story?"

My mother visited Egypt in the late 1970s. This was with her niece Sarah, after Sarah's high-school graduation. Sarah was in a bad place, my mother says, so she took her on a trip. My mother was thirty-four, Sarah seventeen. "Did you have a good time?" I ask. "Oh, we had the best time. We laughed and laughed. I've never laughed so much." "About what?" "Well, Sarah had a mean camel. It tried to bite her. He had to wear a muzzle. And then Sarah's stomach was acting up and she kept drinking Pepto-Bismol and so she had a Pepto-Bismol mustache. And did I ever tell you about 'Tombstone Tooth'?" My mother wrote a book of short stories about a woman named Dinah, a character remarkably similar to her creator. "Tombstone Tooth," an entry in the chronicles, was her elegy to a molar lost in Egypt. The stories were never picked up, though she likes to point out she had an agent who loved them. "I was in the garden of a restaurant on the Nile. I took a bite of pita bread and thought, 'Why is this hard? I'm never coming back here again,' and then I started to chew and realized I was missing a tooth. I was chewing on my own tooth!" And what else did she eat besides the pita? "I had a pigeon-egg omelet." How was it? "It was quite gamey." What was inside it? "Shit, Tom. What do you think? Pigeon eggs!"

∞

When I ask her to send me a copy of "Tombstone Tooth," she hesitates. She has only the one, the file lost somewhere on an ancient computer. I say she could bring it the next time she visits. But when she lands in Tucson and unpacks her meticulous suitcase and sees a library copy of *The Penguin Guide to Ancient Egypt* in my bookcase, she exclaims she forgot to pack it. I believe her about as much as she believes Abby didn't take the bull.

She's right to be suspicious. I do actually have a good eye for stuff. I write down her lines, her jokes, the little acts she puts on. I enter a conversation with her as she enters a room: immediately on the search for treasure to glean, for what nugget or object would look good if used for myself. I know that if I'm there to help her preserve her tomb, I may also be the one who robs it.

Eventually, the Egyptians believed words and images could replace the possessions stored in mastabas. The deceased would be painted at a banquet table, surrounded by friends and family. Small stone statues called *shabtis* replaced sacrificial pets and servants. I imagine Celso breathing a sigh of relief. One could even summon the *akh*, the third part of the soul, by writing a letter to it. This was called *se-akh*: to make the dead live again. Hieroglyphs stood in for actual objects; if you wrote it, the word became the real thing.

When I fly home for Christmas, my mother has the story's pages laid out for me. She doesn't explain why she changed her mind and I don't question the gift. I hold the only copy in my hands, the flimsy three pages she clacked on the computer's keyboard fifteen years ago to write. I know this will be all I'll have left one day and so I read of alter-ego Dinah's being dragged off to the Met with her family, "scooted past all the statues of naked Romans" by a mother trying her best to deny her knowledge of the male anatomy. And the "hard as a rock avocado salad" in the Met garden, and the realization, upon biting down, that "something was amiss in my mouth." I read of the horror as she recognized the broken filling, and how Dinah throws this into the cafeteria fountain, wishing that her tooth feel no pain.

This wish appears over and over again: when Dinah visits the dentist, the improbably named Dr. Needle, and he clamps the anesthetic mask down on her face; when Dinah samples the infamous pita-and-pigeon omelet in Egypt and exclaims, "They put teeth in their bread!"; when she loses the tooth a third time in Brazil, eating "shrimp and garlic" with her husband. And after she last visits Dr. Needle, who amputates the root with "what appeared to be wire cutters," and she walks to the Hudson and tosses the tooth into its waters.

"Tombstone Tooth" is, in part, self-parody. It's another mastaba—self-deprecation as false door, a way to conceal the point where one can be hurt. But it also hides an underlying wish, a plea masked within the inane: to feel no pain in what remains of a life.

I read up on Ancient Egyptian dentistry and learn my mother's wish was not unfounded. Egyptians quite literally lost their bite, dieting on a grain that wore away their teeth's surface and exposed raw nerves. A modern dentist describes their various dental ills as a "pain beyond words." Mummies are found with mouthfuls of cavities, abscesses, and worn-down teeth that caused gangrene and sinus infections so severe they killed.

The remedies for toothache were limited. For a loose tooth, there was honey, ground barley, and ochre. For gingivitis, celery, gum, and sycamore fruit. No real solution existed for cavities, at least no such thing as fillings or drilling tools—only linen soaked in fig juice and cedar oil, packed into the hole to reduce the pain. When no other options were available, the Egyptians used magic. On a few mummies, prosthetic work is found—a loose molar reattached to the mouth by a gold bridge after the patient's death. This was done so that the body would become whole again, the tooth an amulet for the afterlife.

When my mother tells me she summons the dead into her home, she doesn't mention if my father is one of them. She doesn't tell me if she moves over to the couch and invites him to sit once again in his green chair. She never says whether she welcomes him into her bed. When she asks if I ever dream about him, I don't say that I do. I don't say that in these dreams, he is alive and better but she is never there, as if I could only choose one or the other, and in this life I chose her, but in the next I chose him. I don't tell her my memories of them together are disappearing. That while I remember them being in love, I no longer know what that means. That I'm afraid I'll forget her as well when she dies. I too build my mastabas.

Instead, we discuss how much we love her stuff: The desk that belonged to Senator Sumner. The architectural vignette her mother gave her. The Alfonso Ossorio painting. The silver and gold cigarette cases, the rock-and-gem collection, the copper ball I brought back from Arizona, the size and weight of a musket shot. The enameled clocks she makes from scratch. The pictures of the three of us. The iron bull. How many flecks of skin, how many breaths must coat these objects microscopically, ready to unleash a mother of a curse on anyone who doesn't heed her doormat or respect the years her hands must have worried over the fragments that have become her life?

Or her afterlife.

When it comes down to my mother's existence, it depends on which one we're talking about. Consider the old widow, asked to fill out her days within the rooms that were once shared with husband and son, biding her time in an apartment turned mausoleum. The possessions she loves don't provide for any future survival, but her survival right now. They're sustenance not for a hypothetical, storage-unit afterlife, but for the afterlife she's currently within. They are her bond: what keeps her to life, what keeps her alive.

Over the phone these days, her voice slows and occasionally slurs, the same way my father's did in the months before he fell sick. She confuses names as often as she gets them right: I become my aunt, the dog, my father, or my grandfather, based on whatever spirit, animate or inanimate, she's spoken to last. Now I know what her laugh hides: that her voice finally sounds, after all these years, like it could one day die.

There'll come a day when I enter her apartment, lock the door, and search for her in vain. This I know. I'll pick up the phone and scroll through my contacts to call Home or Country and then finally Mom's Cell. And I'll realize she won't pick up any of these, that she's too far away to even regard the flip phone as extraterrestrial.

And when this moment comes, I will open the door and invite her inside. Disregard the doormat, I say, and have a cup of tea. I'll motion to the green chair and she'll sit and her feet will bounce out the same rhythm on the same footstool. She'll drum her hands on her lap and whistle "Celso! Celso!" for the dog. She'll appraise her walls and they will look a bit threadbare. She'll glare—aren't I supposed to be caring for her? I ask what she takes in her tea and, before she can say, "Lots of sugar!" I dust a little ochre, give a squeeze or two of honey. I soak the tea bag in fig and cedar. She takes another look around and spies the cardboard boxes in place of end tables. She'll ask, "My stuff? What have you done with all my stuff?" and I'll tell her truthfully that I let the family in. I had no choice. And that after the plunder, I called Doyle Gallery and arranged a silent auction and many pieces were met with great appreciation. I say if you bind yourself to a substance, then some part of you remains with it. I say look at her and all her dead, how her fingerprints must now ghost so many homes. She seems a bit sad, clapping her hands again for the dog, and so I tell her I have a plan for everything. The house in the country will fetch a good haul, but before it hits the market, I will gather everyone's ashes and find a nice spot out in an open field where there are plenty of birds to talk among themselves and where we will all be happy, no matter who digs us up. I tell her I will keep the iron bull. "And Celso?" she asks, slapping her hands on her thighs again, straining to hear the clatter of incoming toenails on hardwood. I reach down toward my feet and give the black lump a pat. I tell her I'll keep the damn dog. I tell her he and I feel no pain, that we only speak to the dead and animals, but *se-akh*, whenever I miss her, I'll just write down her name and there she'll be.

OVERBURDEN

The story is almost always the same. Every six months or so, I make the trip from Tucson back to my old neighborhood in New York and discover yet another childhood landmark gone. Some landlord or other has forced a beloved store out of business, the rent raised a thousand percent, the real estate handed over to any number of bland chains—a Starbucks, a Janovic Plaza, an HSBC. Worse yet, the building itself has been torn down, or gutted and renovated into condominiums.

I scurry away the names of these lost sites: The Movie Place, its sawdust floors and ladders reaching up to stacks of VHS; Meridiana, where the waiters served children a glass of red wine as long as they were with their parents; La Picola Cucina and its sandwiches drizzled with both olive oil and mayonnaise. With each disappearance, I feel my home reconstitute itself into something I no longer know. These places once formed the texture of a city so that their disappearance

51

signals something perhaps obvious to many: a city loved is a city lost. With enough time, I fear, we become strangers to our own lives, as forgotten as those old stores, serving only as a backdrop for what will become the memories of others who now call our home *home*.

As a result, I've become someone who hates to let things go. Friends tell me I linger. On the street, after dinner or a movie, the light changes from red to green to red, pedestrians curl around our small group, and still I babble on, drawing out goodnights to exasperating lengths. In my free time, I seek the places where you never have to say goodbye. Cemeteries, I'm always hopeful, may prove the one permanent place in a city. Where better for someone like me than a place filled with what we can't bear to leave? Who would ever build a bank or condo or coffee franchise on top of that?

When I moved to Tucson a few years ago, I thought things would be different. Here was a dry and dusty sprawl of a city, so slow-moving and sun-scorched that older laws of geology seemed to hold sway. The strip malls were stuck in the 1970s, peppered with the type of bizarre novelty shops long extinguished in New York: Ken the Bug Guy's Exotic Pet Shop; the Tucson Map and Flag Center; Metaphysics World, a specialty store for "psychics and astrologers." The IHOPs still served pancakes in 1950s A-frame chalets. The city's unofficial motto rallied residents to "Keep Tucson Shitty."

But the longer I stayed, the more this stasis proved a mirage. The downtown underwent its inevitable gentrification, to which I surely contributed. This was deemed a much-needed development. A light-rail opened, university high-rises popped up, and the cash-only dive bar downtown, sandwiched between a World of Beer franchise and a gourmet olive oil shop, announced its closing.

Prior to this in 2004, Pima County decided to build a new courthouse. Its presence would catalyze the downtown's renovation: at seven stories tall and 258,000 square feet, the courthouse would be easily distinguishable from the surrounding warehouses, manufacturing plants, and parking garages. Gone were Coconuts Nightclub, Boyer Motor Co., and Old Pueblo Billiard and Bowling Parlor, long-standing establishments demolished to make way for a new monument to progress and justice.

But the suggested location—the four-way stop where Stone, Alameda, and Toole avenues formed a right triangle—was one of the oldest inhabited sites in the city. Here, traffic lurched its way downtown as the Union Pacific foghorned by every quarter hour on the tracks parallel to Toole, carrying freight for El Paso or L.A., graffiti bubbled across its red and yellow cars. A 1990 Arizona state burial protection law mandated archaeological testing on any site deemed culturally sensitive, and so in 2004 the county hired Statistical Research, Inc., a cultural-resources management firm, to examine the area where the courthouse would now stand. What SRI found was staggering: the remains of National Cemetery, unmarked and undesignated, containing over 1,300 human remains to parse, remove, and repatriate.

∞

In 1864, U.S. government agent J. Ross Browne arrived in Tucson and sniffed his nose at it: "A city of mud boxes," he wrote. "Dingy and dilapidated, cracked and baked into a composite of dust and filth, barren of verdure, parched, naked, and grimly desolate in the glare of a southern sun."

Browne was one of a wave of white settlers to arrive in Tucson at that time. After the Gadsden Purchase made Southern Arizona a United States territory in 1854, men and women flocked to the predominantly Mexican outpost, categorizing and dividing the land already inhabited by Native American tribes for over a millennium. Between 1848 and 1880, Tucson's population shot from 760 to more than seven thousand.

With this increase, certain necessities arose. One was a space for the dead. Just before the Civil War, residents began digging graves in a plot of land bordering Stone Avenue; from 1860 to 1881, roughly two thousand burials formed National Cemetery.

National also wouldn't have suited J. Ross Browne's tastes. The Sonoran caliche made digging a maddening task. Proper burial custom required only that the body rest deeply enough that its bones were not visible. Adobe walls ran around the cemetery to keep out wild animals and deter inhabitants from abandoning corpses without proper burial. Civilian graves were dug inside and outside the walls, edged up against public outhouses and trash heaps. The *Arizona Daily Star* called National Cemetery "the general dump ground of the city," a place filled with everything from dead rats to a dead horse, the ground so littered with half-dug graves that "if a pedestrian happens that way after dark he is likely to fall into one of the numerous pits and get his neck broken." Charles D. Poston, the state's first congressman and the so-called Father of Arizona, attended an officer's funeral at National in 1881 and lamented that it "gave the people a sad opportunity to witness the neglect and desecration which rests upon the mural monuments of the brave dead." "Cannot something be done?" he asked.

Something was. National's civilian section closed in 1875 and its military section in 1881, shortly after Poston's visit. In 1884, a notice ran in the *Daily Star* that a Dr. W. J. White would exhume the remains and move them to nearby cemeteries. The neighboring real estate had been sold to the railroad, and the city anticipated a more profitable use for the land than a graveyard. For those families who could afford it, the dead were transported north to Court Cemetery. For those who couldn't, the dead stayed put. Like any constituency of voiceless residents, cemetery occupants fell victim to zoning. By 1900 the land became residential, and then, over the next sixty years, businesses took over piece by piece. No external signs of the cemetery remained, though the number of accidental exhumations—the spades that struck bone in service of foundation and latrine—spiked.

No longer in use, National Cemetery was classified as defunct. The category on first consideration seems puzzling. Does the space of the dead itself die? What happens when the land meant for preservation rubs up against the space marked out for the living?

∞

On a late summer's day in downtown Tucson, just past lunch, the construction site for the new Pima County Courthouse is hushed. No heavy machinery rumbles; no trucks beep in reverse; the busy yells of workers have ceased.

Alone in the still air, the county courthouse appears almost complete. Its seven stories of glass and steel reflect nothing but sky. Little evidence remains that here one of the largest mass exhumations in American history took place.

One Friday afternoon, I locked my bike and walked along the chain-link fence running around the new courthouse, hoping to visit what I could. Unlike a cemetery, a construction site does not exactly welcome visitors. Sundt Construction, the contractor who won the bidding for the job, had posted the usual signs along its fence: VIOLATORS WILL BE PROSE-CUTED; NOT HIRING AT THIS JOBSITE; NO TRESPASSING, HARD HAT AREA. A three-foot poster of the model worker was stapled to the fence, each piece of protective gear labeled and explained.

Then I saw another sign: VISITORS MUST CHECK IN AT SUNDT OFFICES. This seemed an implicit invitation—it didn't specify which type of visitor must check in, only that this obligation awaited if you considered yourself one. And wasn't I visiting? I walked to where the fence's gates were pulled back, took a look around, and stepped inside.

Not ten steps later and I came face-to-face with a worker, the first I had seen. He was in full compliance with the poster on the fence—orange vest, hard hat, safety glasses, and the name *Jason* stitched across his Dickies shirt. I told him I was looking for the Sundt office and was hoping to take a tour. He asked why. "I just found out this was a cemetery," I said, and suddenly afraid that idle interest was not enough, that I must have some personal stake in the matter, I mentioned that my great-grandfather had been buried here. Did he think it was possible to pay my respects? It was a lie, but it worked. Jason nodded and pointed to a trailer behind me: "Tell them what you told me and I don't see why not."

It should come as no surprise that a cemetery once sat in the center of the city. "The city of the dead is the forerunner, almost the core, of every living city," writes Lewis Mumford, the architectural critic. The burial of their dead encouraged prehistoric humans to occupy permanent sites, so much so that the philosopher Hans-Georg Gadamer argued burial "is perhaps the fundamental phenomenon of becoming human." Metropolis and necropolis are obverse and reverse; a city grows and so too must its dead. The stores that cycle in and out of my old neighborhood in New York are really reminders that the people in the apartments above live and die and are shuffled out as well.

Walling off a space for the dead then becomes a civic function, no different than providing the infrastructure for sewage, electricity, or running water. At the same time, a cemetery is more than just functional: it disposes of the dead, yet also provides them a home. It's built *of* the dead, but *for* the living. Visitors—potential inhabitants, after all—both pay for and provide its present sustenance as well as supply its literal future. Think of it as the grandparent who has you by the ear—a cemetery needs an audience to pass along its memories of a city's past occupants, yet it's also there to send a message, a basic inevitable truth: a city of the living one day turns into a city of the dead. Though we all die, with the proper record-keeping and a bit of endowment, we might not all be forgotten.

I climbed the steps to the Sundt Construction office, a white plywood trailer on the vacant lot. A woman looked up from her desk when I opened the door. Nervous, I spat out the story I concocted on the walk over. "My great-grandfather just up and moved to Tucson," I told her. "I think he traveled by train to prospect. But he died and I was told he was buried here." The woman cut me off before I could hash out any particulars of his death. "They did all the reburials at Fort Huachuca and All Faiths," she said, as if she had heard this before. "The most you can do is see where he would have been. But you'll have to ask Ben first."

Ben, it turned out, had just walked in behind me. The site foreman, he seemed the kind of man whose curfew you wouldn't want to break when taking his daughter to prom. His face was more saddle than skin, his buzz cut an extension of his chin's stubble. I followed him into his office and he stood behind his desk. "So you want a tour? Can't do it. You need the proper equipment." He pointed down to my canvas shoes and up at my bare head. "Steel-toed boots, safety glasses, a hard hat. It's a safety-code thing. Walking around, you never know what might fall on you."

I nodded and said I understood, that I had some steel-toed

boots but they were a three-mile bike ride away. Still I lingered and Ben didn't kick me out. I took this as another invitation. I worked my way through a revision of my story—how my great-grandfather abandoned my great-grandmother on the East Coast and wound up in Tucson only to die shortly thereafter, how I had never known this until my aunt mentioned it the other day, how this was the last shred of him I had left.

Ben sat down, took off his hard hat, and ran his thumb and forefinger along his forehead. "Was he military?" he asked.

I paused, considering whether this was ever in the cards for a family member of mine. "I don't think so," I said.

"And this was your *great*-grandfather?" Ben let that hang in the air. I look like someone whose great-grandfather had been born in 1900 at the latest.

"Well, great-great really. It's just easier to say *great* and mean *great-great*."

Ben nodded and opened a file on his desktop. He traced his finger along an aerial photograph of the construction site, outlining the perimeter where National Cemetery once lay and the three construction sections it had become—courthouse, parking garage, front lot—each with a swath of overturned land next to it like a smudged finger painting. Then he pointed to the roof of a brown building in the southwest corner. "There are still bodies underneath there. That's the only part that wasn't excavated." He stopped and thought for a second. "I'll have to show you round myself, seeing as you don't have the right gear. Just keep your sunglasses on and grab those." He pointed to a bin full of hard hats and orange vests, the proper safety equipment that had been sitting behind me the entire time.

∞

It turns out a defunct cemetery is a fairly common occurrence. A state of rest has its transitions like any other. If graves are houses of the dead, then they too must submit to the practical—the mortgages, payments, and installments needed to retain a desired, inhabitable space.

In Tucson, there was the smattering of two-thousand-year-old burials at the base of Sentinel Peak, the saguaro-strung hill just west of the interstate emblazoned with the University of Arizona's red, white, and blue *A*. Then there was Presidio San Agustín, built by Mexican settlers in 1776, where more than a thousand bodies still remain downtown, and where each November thousands of costumed gatherers parade along Alameda Street to celebrate All Souls Procession, Tucson's version of Día de los Muertos. On All Souls, the city turns upside down and the living dress as the dead until one does not know which is which. People build floats with giant skeletons and scythes, creep down darkened streets on stilts, paint skulls on their faces, and carry pictures of dead family members. A crowd of strangers comes together in embodiment of what they've lost, marching over the San Agustín cemetery underneath.

Then there was Court Cemetery, the graveyard that replaced National's civilian portion in 1875, a half mile north of the railroad tracks. It's a cemetery described in an 1877 *Arizona Weekly Citizen* editorial as a "drear, bleak, desolate place," where it would be "cruelty in the highest degree to compel parents, kindred, and friends to entomb and take final leave of their dear departed ones." Though the cemetery closed in 1909 and homes sprouted over it by 1915, up to six thousand bodies still remain unmarked and underground in the residential neighborhood of Dunbar/Spring. In Dunbar/Spring, a post hole for a mailbox strikes a grave; excavation for a sewer line yields two coffins stacked one on top of another; an eleven-foot-long, half-foot-wide crack appears in the earth after a rainstorm and when the earth falls apart, it opens up two more graves layered on top of each other like bunk beds, the dead bleeding into the living and the once defunct springing improbably back to life.

As Ben and I walked around to the dirt lot in back, he told me that the genealogy bug had bit him as well. He Googled his last name a few years ago to discover that his ancestors came from Chihuahua, Mexico. "My own great-grandpa," he said with some pride, "was a Jesuit priest. He traveled up to Sonora, met a Native woman, and that was it." He winked. "No more priesthood." Ben searched his great-grandfather's name and found a match in Hermosillo, Mexico. "My great-grandfather's brother's great-grandson." He tried to puzzle out the connection. "Now let's see, what does that make us?" He paused. "Cousins, I guess," he laughed. "It gets tricky, you know?"

I nodded in commiseration and told him, truthfully this time, that on my father's side of the family in Brazil, my uncle had recently exhumed my grandfather and had him cremated after more than half a century in a cemetery in Petropolis, a small mountain city an hour's ride from Rio de Janeiro. My uncle sprinkled my grandfather's ashes alongside my grandmother's at the *sitio*, the house my grandparents built in the 1950s and where my father and his siblings were raised. My uncle did this not just to reunite both his parents on the same land but also to receive a healthy sum from selling the plot.

What I told Ben, however, wasn't as simple as all that. My uncle had exhumed his father and scattered his ashes a year or so after what was left of our family buried handfuls of my grandmother's ashes at the *sitio*, a little at a time, each in a particular spot she loved: beneath the birds-of-paradise by the pool, by the Adirondack chair my father had brought down from New York to assemble, at the base of the jaboticaba trees down the drive.

But my uncle also wanted to save the *sitio* and so he bought the place, using most of the inheritance he received from his mother after fifty-nine less-than-patient years of waiting. His plan was admirable: if he preserved the land, he would preserve the memory of those people who also loved it yet could no longer care for it: his parents and my father. Like my uncle, I too regarded the *sitio* as a magical place—growing up, I would make the twelve-hour flight down to Rio with my parents, spend a few days in the city's swelter, and then climb the winding route through the mountains and jungle until we entered what seemed another, more vertiginous world— *bromélias* and *cachoeiras* springing from cliffs, clouds curling over mountains to bring sudden thunder, a breeze that, at the right time of night, could rustle your bones. Like my uncle,

I daydreamed that, when I grew older, I would end up there as well.

Yet my uncle was also in equal measure a fool. Soon after he bought the *sitio*, he borrowed even more money he couldn't return and found himself forced to sell the house and everything that came with it. He lost the garden, the birds-of-paradise, the greenhouse, the hummingbirds. He lost the dirt soccer field out back where my grandfather used to practice his shot put. He lost the orange and lime trees, the fruit growing on the bark of the jaboticabas, the dark marble berries to be turned into jam. He lost the dead wasps scumming the surface of the pool and the spiderwebs stretched taut across the back walkway, stronger than fishing line. And I lost the back ridge where my father fell thirty years ago and broke his ankle. I lost the dusted-over Ping-Pong table and the television where our family watched Baggio shank one over the net in '94. I lost Maria Comprida, the mountain my grandmother would gaze up at every time she sat in the Adirondack chair my father positioned for her, the mountain whose outline I tattooed onto my forearm so that I may never lose it again.

What saddens me most is not that I had allowed myself to believe one of my uncle's long drawn-out flights of fancy, but that there'll come a moment when whoever buys the place stops at the foot of the jaboticabas and notices the overturned dirt, appearing as a darker stain than the rest of the deeply watered and lushly green earth. The impostor (for who else could this person be who bought the house my grandparents built?) will dig through the dirt and rock, and then through my grandmother's and grandfather's commingled ashes, some volcanic and fine, some coarser and chipped. Then the new owner, planning some grander landscaping, will prepare to yank everything out by its roots but first sift through the earth, letting his fingers run through it to wonder, if only for a moment, what ghosts might now be strangers in their own home.

Ben and I walked behind the courthouse and stood at the edge of a pit, mounds of bulldozed earth piled around us. A worker, a lanky older white man, walked past us carrying two buckets of dirt, his shoulders sagging under the weight.

A crane sat idly on the far side of the hole, and beyond that ran Sixth Avenue's traffic. This would be the courthouse's parking garage, the only structure left to build. "We're standing where they uncovered most of the bodies," Ben said. "So chances are your great-grandpa was buried here." I nodded solemnly and peeked over the edge.

Ben said he had heard stories from the excavation team about the bones they found: a mother holding a baby on either side of her; a skeleton with bullet holes in the rib cage and sternum. "It's quite a structure," Ben said, looking up at the courthouse. "You know why they had to exhume here? The foundation's twenty feet deep, deeper than any other building built before here. We'd have poured concrete onto all those bodies."

Ben turned back to the pit. I wanted to ask him what he thought about working here, whether he felt unsettled, whether he too supposed himself a transgressor. The city had decided, after all, to bring in a priest to bless the site before construction began.

As much as graves provide a second home for the dead, it's a home we don't want them to leave. Look at the beginnings of any burial practice and you will see the steps taken by the living to stop the dead from returning. The heavy stones and menhirs first used in Western Europe don't just mark a burial place; they physically keep the dead from rising. In France up until the late eighteenth century, bodies suspected of being likely to come back to life were disinterred and decapitated. To prevent the dead's resurrection, people have burned them, eaten them, carried their ashes in small pouches around their necks. They have rubbed out the dead's footprints so they could not find their way home, blindfolded corpses and led them out from their houses to their graveyards by unfamiliar routes. They have sealed up the dead body's orifices to keep the soul from leaving. Corpses have been tied down, their bones broken, barriers of fire lit between grave and town. Families have urinated along the doorways of their houses so that if a ghost were to enter, he would drink the urine, spit it out, and leave. People have danced on graves to crush the body underneath. Even the Dance of Death, that Middle Ages allegory on the universality of mortality, was meant to tamp down the earth so the dead couldn't seep out.

We miss the dead, we mourn them, we dress in their visage and try many means to preserve their memory—but is all this done because we want to bring them back to life or because, in some sense, we want to keep them dead? To remember someone is not the same, after all, as wishing for that someone's return. Perhaps a grave is just a means of assuaging guilt, a way of fooling us into thinking we can hold on to a place or person, so that when the neighborhood sewer line is struck or the courthouse built or a house's new occupants decide to do some light work around the yard, the earth does not open upon our ancestors only for us to hear of the wrongs we've done and the ways in which we've left them behind.

Before Ben and I walked back, he pointed across the lot to the building from the bird's-eye photograph. "That's where they didn't dig. Check it out when you leave. There are bodies still buried there. Just slip in the alleyway up Stone."

A year after I visited National Cemetery, I met John Hall. Doughy, invariably friendly, and dressed in baggy, waterproof clothes as if just returned from the field, he waited for me in his office down and around a long corridor of SRI's headquarters in East Tucson. After a chain of intermediaries and months of over-the-phone stonewalling from the SRI secretary, I had found him, John Hall, the lead field archaeologist for the excavation at National. His office had no windows. A map of the excavation site, each burial a slightly pinched rectangle, was tacked to his wall.

"I'm always happy to reminisce," John said, swiveling his chair between me and his desktop, where he had pulled up photos from the excavation. "This was probably the biggest project I'll ever have in my life."

SRI's excavation was a massive, painstaking, year-and-a-half-long undertaking. In order to find a grave, a backhoe stripped away foundation and overburden—the layer of rock and soil overlying the cemetery—and then sifted through the dirt for bones. John and a team of seventy parsed the dry, stubborn caliche to catch sight of the darker dirt and decomposed wood that indicated grave and coffin. To reach the densest part of the cemetery, they dug through sewers and building foundations, cut gas lines and water pipes, and scattered burials. Upon finding remains, SRI took cranial measurements to determine each skeleton's ancestry. They collected what artifacts remained in the graves—rosary beads, crosses, buttons made of metal, wood, and shell—and recorded each burial's position so that its arrangement could be recreated upon repatriation.

Yet, for all that, SRI couldn't determine who was who. "The county hired us to clear the site," John shrugged, "and so that's what we did." For expediency's sake, they sacrificed steps such as DNA testing that otherwise would have been taken. Although Tucson's Catholic diocese kept records of the buried, it didn't record who was buried where, so only a few remains could be identified. These rare successes depended on the right confluence of events—two skeletons with bullet wounds in their chests were only identified when a slog through Tucson's 1870s crime headlines turned up an obituary for a shopkeeper and his wife shot to death in the armed robbery of their store.

The most telling material was found in what else the excavation exposed: centuries-old trash; a prehistoric pit house with a streetlight's foundation running through the middle of it; a dog's skeleton buried underneath a house's foundation. Privies and outhouses proved especially rich. John and his team dug shafts twenty feet deep and at the bottom, they would chance upon a perfectly preserved newspaper or a grocery receipt reading *pigs, bacon grease, flour.*

"It was like arranging a tapestry," John said.

This seemed a funny way to describe the process. Comparing the layers of a city to an intricate weave of textiles meant to create a larger, complex representation of a scene is fairly intuitive, and it makes sense to juxtapose the skill and care needed to excavate so rich an archaeological site as National with the artistic craft and precision necessary to fashion a tapestry. But what's most interesting is that a tapestry is primarily ornamental: it's a wall hanging, a furniture covering, something to look at. Does the same then hold true for National? A cemetery memorializes and archaeology studies the dead, but while both honor their subject, they value it in often-contradictory forms. The question of how to properly handle the dead—who, despite all those who claim to speak for them, stay silent in the matter—remains unanswerable.

When SRI excavated the cemetery, they consulted with both the Tohono O'odham Nation and Los Descendientes, the heritage groups that claimed cultural affinity with the cemetery's inhabitants. Los Descendientes approved of the plan for exhumation—they wanted to know everything they possibly could about their ancestors and considered the current burial state unsuitable; any information was of value to them, and members would often visit John Hall at the site, asking him about what had been found. The Tohono O'odham Nation resisted that idea and didn't want the burial site disturbed at all: what happened at National Cemetery, to them, was sacrilege.

Once the excavation was complete, the problem still remained of what to do with the bodies. From May 2009 till June 2010, Pima County exhumed, transported, and reburied individual remains. Civilians went to All Faiths Cemetery, military to Fort Huachuca, and the thirty-six Native American remains to the Tohono O'odham Nation. Each cemetery held its own rededication ceremony. More than two thousand people attended the military reburial on Armed Forces Day. Governor Jan Brewer gave a speech; Gabby Giffords, district congresswoman at the time, rode her motorcycle there.

The designated name for this process was "repatriation," a sending back to "one's own country." The term raises the question: what constitutes one's country, and who decides those borders? The exhumation was spun so that the bodies were now returning to their "true home," as if the same thing hadn't been said about those early Tucsonans when they were buried in their *first* final resting place. Add to this the irony that these remains were upended by a courthouse—a structure that, at least in the great state of Arizona and its SB-1070 laws, symbolizes a legal system used to unfairly target and deny the citizenship of many descendants of those remains—and *repatriation* starts to take on a more ominous ring. If the exhumation at National Cemetery reclaimed a sense of culture and heritage, it also asserted possession of the land. Just as I claimed a long-lost ancestor, Pima County claimed to honor a forgotten cultural lineage to access a desired site.

When my tour with Ben had ended, I handed him the hard hat and vest and made my way down Stone Avenue. I disappeared once again into the emptiness of the street and the slow, comfortable rhythm of traffic. When I reached the L-shaped alleyway he had pointed out, I ducked into it. The whole expanse lay in front of me: the pit that would become a parking garage, the seven stories of glass and steel, and the city beyond that, dropping and lengthening until it reached the Catalina Mountains, distant but sharply etched. From the site, a hammer knocked a calm and repeated ring. The same lanky man emerged from behind a dirt mound carrying the same two buckets. Contrails shoelaced across the sky. The freight train would pass behind Toole in a minute.

I turned around to face the building. It was the squat brown office of the school superintendent. In the alleyway, a line of violet spray paint ran around the building's perimeter, perforated like a cut-here diagram. Someone had spray-painted *SRI Excavation* on the outside of this line and then several arrows pointing in the direction of the courthouse. Here was the border, the dividing line between repatriation and remains.

By 1900, fourteen middle-class residences were built on the spot where I stood. Unlike National's occupants, those who lived there have names: George Whomes, dentist, and his wife, Adah; John Brown, a rancher, and his wife, Dolores; George Cheyney, the postmaster, and his wife, Anne. While National Cemetery represented one of the most diverse cemeteries ever exhumed in the U.S., there were now only three non-Anglo-American residents on that land. They were Nicolasa Antonio, the Native American servant of George and Anne Cheyney; Matilda Sturis, the Mexican servant of George and Adah Whomes; and Clara Antonio, whom the records sometimes state as Mexican, sometimes as Native American, but always the servant of Phillip and Elizabeth Brennan.

Before John Brown died in 1914, he had a fear much the same as my own about the *sitio*: that the paving of Stone Avenue would destroy the beloved mulberry trees he had planted in back of his house. Old John Brown made no mention of what his own house might have paved, or what the mulberry trees might themselves have uprooted.

We don't know this for certain, but I'm willing to bet that when it came to his mulberry trees, John Brown wasn't thinking of Dora Scribner Miller, a woman who arrived in Tucson in 1885 at the age of six and who, when asked by the *Tucson Citizen* in 1953 if she remembered National Cemetery, delivered an account in opposition to every other newspaper's negative report: "Why, that place was an old cemetery when we first came to Tucson. It was one of the first things we saw when we got off the train—lots of mesquite and catclaw with little paths through the trees to the graves. There were always candles burning, and day or night you could see someone there saying a rosary."

I cannot move past this when it comes to National Cemetery's exhumation: that we can match the names and locations of the people above, but not those who lived below. The cemetery Dora Scribner Miller remembered ended up a forgotten space—not obverse and reverse, not a city of the dead and a city of the living, but just one more strata of history in the underground cross section, another archaeological feature alongside the utility lines and gas mains and water pipes and cement foundations, the overburden you dig through to get to what you really want. I had hoped a cemetery would prove more special, that it could carry ghosts. But a grave may very well prove less illuminating than a privy and the newspaper used to wipe someone's nineteenth-century ass.

What bothered me about National is what ultimately bothers me about all cemeteries. I arrive at each one hoping to find permanence, only to discover that within their promise of preservation lies the hint that they allow us to forget. I hate saying goodbye. But this isn't so much the pain of parting as it is the fear of forgetting. To deal with grief, to survive what would otherwise be too sharp-edged, we must allow a dullness to take root. By staking memory to a place, we absolve ourselves of its full weight; the bookmark replaces the finger that might have been kept on the page. I try my best to remember—I walk down Alameda Street on a warm November night with a skull painted on my face and my father's photo in hand; I daydream about the table at Meridiana where I am once again fifteen years old and, in between the calamari and the *salmone al affumicato*, my father orders me a glass of red wine. Still I know there remains an eagerness for oblivion within the memorials I create, a desire to wash over everything like the mountains in the distance. A city buries its dead just so it can keep on living. Whether exhumed or not, a grave doesn't maintain what's been lost so much as it concedes the ghost is never really coming back.

THE PATH TO THE SAINTS

In 2008, microbiologists discovered two new species of bacteria growing within the Catacombs of Priscilla in Rome. This discovery thrilled the admittedly narrow set of biologists, since the bacteria's existence contained useful keys on how to better preserve the underground networks. Yet the bacteria also ate away at the catacomb walls, staining the volcanic rock white, causing minerals to dry out until they became a fine powder, an efflorescence like granulated flour or ground bone. Their presence created a dilemma. What is to be done when the only thing left alive in a place also destroys it?

I lived in the north of Rome in the fall of 2006. Tourist maps cut off this part of the city, the neighborhood outside the ancient walls where the Romans buried their dead. I was studying abroad for a semester in college and so "lived" is probably the wrong word. A friend once said you only lived in a place if you received mail there, and I did not. Instead, I rolled my suitcase into a small, windowless bedroom for a homestay with Paolo, an architect in his late thirties. Paolo lived by himself in an apartment his mother owned on a street named after Vivaldi. He rented the extra room to students. I was one of a dozen or so Americans that had stayed with him over the years, though he did not speak much English, and I, despite having wanted to go to Rome for three years, knew no Italian.

Paolo, by his own account, was a melancholy guy. He listened to Tom Waits and Fabrizio de André at night and, since architectural work was slim in the Italian economy, drafted freelance designs at his desk. He owned a computer from the 1990s that he never turned on. He had curly, pipe-cleaner hair swept back from his forehead, giving the impression he might bald someday. He looked like the villain of some movie I couldn't remember. I was very nervous to meet him, and the first thing I did was to explain, with demonstrative hand gestures, that I did not like George W. Bush.

Paolo was disciplined. He trained for half-marathons in the park and timed his pasta with a stopwatch. He allowed himself a baby can of Coke with dinner each night. *Mio vizio*, he'd say, pointing to the can. We ate together at his kitchen table while watching histrionic Italian game shows where contestants had to choose between the unknown contents of large wooden boxes and follow sets of seemingly arbitrary, inconsequential rules. "I hate this show," Paolo would say. Then he'd go on to explain its rules to me.

Shortly after I moved in with Paolo, my father became unexpectedly sick and began dying, hospitalized first in Rio de Janeiro and then New York City. I did a lot of walking around those months, beating the same path between school and Paolo's apartment, waiting for bad news via expensive cell phone calls. I watched old women walk around my neighborhood and grew furious at them for their health. I'd wander down to Villa Borghese, where I'd stare at the Bernini sculptures alongside the other tourists: dutiful Aeneas with Anchises on his back, carrying his aged father out of Troy. I stopped buying into the system that many buy into: that bad things aren't supposed to happen to you because you haven't agreed to this narrative. I'd circle the highways that ringed the city, lost in the middle of the night until the metros opened in the morning. I'd walk back to Paolo's house, sleep an hour, then wake up and walk to my elementary Italian class.

In short, I had very little mooring me to real life except for my host. He asked how I was doing. He'd make me speak in Italian and then let me switch back to English when I got tired. He'd moon his eyes out to let me know he understood what I was trying to say. When I did the same, he laughed and called me Mr. Bean, the Rowan Atkinson character from another stupid show we both had watched. He'd share his little can of Coke with me. Afterward, when I fell asleep at 9 p.m., he'd wake me up so we could get gelato. Somehow we understood each other—as if language were only a river whose rocks and mud we had to wade our way through.

Paolo's house stood a fifteen-minute walk from the Catacombs of Priscilla. Wealthy patrons in Ancient Rome built these catacombs beneath their property in exchange for sainthood. Priscilla, my neighborhood benefactress and the wife of a Roman politician, donated her land in the late second century CE.

Roman catacombs were originally designed like a fishbone, a central spine with galleries jackknifing off on either side like ribs. As burials increased, their structures grew more complicated until, by the fifth century, with its maze of honeycombs and orthogonals, a map of the catacombs would have looked like the molecule you memorize for an organic chemistry test. *Fossores*, the catacomb diggers, had to ensure their tunnels corresponded with property lines overhead. When they reached their outer limits, the *fossores* simply dug down. Priscilla descends some three stories deep and is thirteen kilometers long; if you stretched it out, you could walk to the Colosseum and back and still not have exhausted its paths.

As the catacombs grew, it became more difficult to determine who was buried where. To ease navigation, *fossores* left *itinera ad sanctos*—paths to the saints—in the tunnels, skylights that guided visitors down corridors until they reached a martyr's tomb. Families left small markers by graves, statues or trinkets of little value. They carved epitaphs as well, brief messages imploring visitors not to disturb the body, like the NO RADIO sign taped to a parked car: "He lived thirty years. In peace." *"Aeternae memoriae."* "Not a seventh part of what once existed."

I spoke to my father twice while I was in Rome. Paralyzed on his right side, he was no longer capable of forming real speech. Only a breath and then a syllable: a "T—" that could not become *Tom.* On the other end, when I spoke, I wanted to shout out loud like the game show host Paolo and I watched every night, eager to window dress the Italian I was learning. I wanted to parade the words, the short, staccato, twinned syllables. *Ho dimenticato tutto mi Italiano.* "I've forgotten all my Italian." *Sono stanco!* "I am tired!" Or the words when wanting to leave a crowded bus: *Scusi, scusi, permesso!* "Excuse me, excuse me, I have to get out of here!"

We visited the Catacombs of Priscilla on class trips. The tour guides showed us the mosaic on the ceilings of women leading the Eucharist, smudged over so that the women appeared as men. God forbid the historical record reveal female priests. On the walls, there was a censored Medusa's head, her Gorgon curls whited out, the snaky ends now a mess of ringletted hair, your garden-variety, photoshopped saint. All over the catacombs lay the evidence that people reconstituted bodies to better suit a message.

I stood at the back on these trips, bored and waiting for the tour to be over. I traced the electric cabling that ran along the tops of the tunnels. I thought how I should probably leave Rome and move back home with my father. I wondered why I did not. The tour guides told us about the walls, the soft volcanic tufa the Romans initially believed bees nested within, walls that now were filled with tombs, *loculi* stacked three or four high like bunk beds. I thought of the rehab ahead, of how my father's body and mind would be permanently changed. I thought of all he would lose. I realized I did not want to go back because my father would not be my father anymore and, when I knew this, I told myself he'd be better off dead. I was tired, I said, and so was he and it was okay to give up. The tour guides told us that when it grew too hot in the summer, Priscilla would bring her family down into the catacombs to eat their meals. I thought how if you thinned out Paolo's face, gave him a darker head of hair, and cast him in dim-enough light, you could say: there goes my father.

Paolo and I ran in the park together. We visited architectural museums and drank Birra Moretti with his friends. We hung our laundry from the clothesline out the window. Ours was an easy domesticity. He cooked and I did the dishes. He taught me how to make a good tomato sauce (a pinch of sugar to offset the seeds' bitterness), to sauté couscous directly in the pan with chicken and olive oil and red wine vinegar. He weighed his pasta in grams and tossed it into the frying pan for a minute to mix with the sauce. He showed me if you cooked Bolognese in *conchiglie*, the meat would hide in the shell to form an ad hoc dumpling. He told me not to eat so fast when he saw me scarf it all down.

If I counted the hours, I might find I spent more time with Paolo in four months than with my father in the previous four years. My father worked long hours—in the lab from nine in the morning to nine at night—and I had a lock on my door at the age when I would use it. Then came college. At some point, I don't really know where the time went. One day there was a man and the next a scratch on the wall lamenting this was not a seventh part of what once existed.

One night, Paolo and I ran into each other as we both entered his building. We rode the elevator, one of those small old European things with folding doors and a metal grate that shuts so fast it might take off your foot. We stood almost touching but did not speak. As the elevator cranked itself up, the moment was outside enough of our usual contexts that it made us strangers. Suddenly Paolo became someone I didn't know at all, someone I didn't understand. We had been speaking the wrong words all along. I had a moment of B-movie paranoia and thought, ridiculously, how he could pull a knife out from his jacket and stab me in the chest. He really did look like the villain from a movie I had seen long ago.

I was wrong, of course. Still, I've never felt that way about someone I know. He had become a symbol, and that consequently meant he was wide open for interpretation.

∞

Other nights, I'd come home to find Paolo eating potato chips and drinking his little can of Coke at the kitchen table. His blueprints and drafts lay untouched on his desk. "That's your dinner?" I asked him the first night I found him this way. "Yes, usually," he said. When you live alone, he said, you let yourself eat like that, you let yourself go.

"Why not get back together with your ex-girlfriend? Why not have kids?" I asked him, the same way I ask single people now if they want a cat. I thought if he could care for me, he could care for others. The two of them were friends and she sometimes came over to the apartment in the afternoon. She seemed as melancholy as he did. "Boh!" Paolo exclaimed and turned up his hands, the sound he made when he did not want to tell you the answer. Then he bugged his eyes out, spread his mouth into a smile. "Never be friends with your ex-girlfriend," he said. And he rubbed his eyes and said there was no point, no, he'd never have kids, there was no point.

The weekend before I left, Paolo and I biked along Via Appia, the ancient road that connected Rome to Brindisi, the road where the catacombs were first rediscovered.

We bought a baguette, some cheese and salami, and a bottle of Coke. I couldn't bike well, it being years since my father and I rode in the park, and Paolo would wait for me, pulled to the cobblestones' side as I wobbled along. We ate on a grassy hill by the road. I didn't know it, but we were following the ancient pagan tradition of dining with ancestors on Sundays, just as Priscilla must have done.

The hill was near the hollow where a millennium ago an earthquake or a landslide opened a shaft in a vineyard and exposed a path down into the catacombs. Here, explorers first mapped the catacombs and followed *itinera ad sanctos* until they reached saints' bodies. They plundered these, substituting anonymous skeletons for martyrs, rearranging epitaphs to create sanctified graves, the human body once again reconstituted to serve a message.

After we ate, I asked Paolo where he saw himself in ten years. "Ten years?" he asked, smiling because it was a silly question he didn't know how to answer. "I'll be dead," he said.

That was nine years ago now.

According to scholars, the epitaphs left next to the catacomb tombs were "rarely very communicative." They "provoke rather than satisfy curiosity," there not so much to tell us who a person was as to remind us not to disturb that person's rest.

What's curious about catacomb epitaphs is how precisely, how assiduously, they record the age of the dead. They measure lives down to the hour. One fragment in Priscilla reads: "To his dearest wife, with whom I lived so many years, six months, three days, and fifteen hours." And another: "Five years, two months, six days, and six hours."

This record-keeping is touching, if not baffling. Why be so Swiss about time? But maybe this is the point—knowing how much will be lost, and the expanse that will be slowly eaten away, perhaps the only way to recognize a person is to acknowledge the days we had with them, to count the exact moments and believe that an extra six hours a millennium ago mattered as much as all the ones in between.

The morning I left Rome, we were running so late that Paolo had to push me on board the train to Fiumicino. Earlier, he handed me a note in Italian, at the end of which he wrote: *quando una porta si chiude, un'altra si apre.* "When one door closes, another opens." That's a cliché, I know, the simplest solution to an architectural problem, but it was what I wanted to hear. I don't know exactly what he meant, but I wondered if, through the vagaries of language, he intended it the same way I took it: that when my father died, I found him.

Now I do not preserve the memory of my father so much as the memory of my losing him. His cold hands on my cheek after he came home from work. His hunch over the dinner plate my mother left out for him, the pasta and sauce always cooked separately. The way his knees have become my knees— so knobby that when I sleep on my side I need an airplane pillow to soften the bones. How he and I must look like bodies in their *loculi* that way.

To write about a memory, another saying goes, kills that memory. An act of preservation is an act of distortion. Just ask those explorers: when we get close enough to someone, we end up with someone else.

That's fine, I guess. If my father's no longer a person, then he's a place where a person once was. A void, a quarry, a hollow. Material to carve into—tufa, soft porous rock, the ash sprung from volcanoes. Bacteria stained white, a structure slowly turned to ruin by the being that most wants to keep it alive.

The catacomb epitaphs, in their mixture of Greek and Latin, were some of the earliest iterations of the Italian Paolo and I pidgined our way through.

A funny thing happens when you're able to communicate a simple phrase in another language to someone else. It's as if you then know that person better than you've known any other. As if the precision needed for those few words was more than you could muster with all the words in your own tongue. As if to say anything at all is a hard-won power, microscopic and microbial, persistent and painstaking and all too slow to be seen.

Sometimes I search online for Paolo, hoping that in the intervening years he turned on his computer and signed up for wireless. I search hoping he's still alive. But though I come close, I can find no trace of him—there's a Paolo Boni who's a lawyer in Rome, another who's an architect in Milan. I run through images but do not see his face. I stop for a second or two—there's someone his age, laughing or smiling, his arms around his friends—and I wonder if I've gotten it all wrong, if this is actually him and I'm remembering someone else.

∞

Other times I go back and look through Google Maps and zoom in real close to Via Vivaldi. I click on the chubby little yellow man and drop him onto the blue line of street. Suddenly, there I am in the digital flesh, a little herky-jerky, dizzy from my bird's-eye fall as I swivel my fat yellow head around the streets. But once I gain my footing, I start to whirl around, first slowly then faster, 180 then 360, patient, swiveling my cursor, honing in not on the pavement or cars or storefronts or angles but on the people—searching their blurred, anonymous faces in the long-shot hope that there's an outline or a semblance of a body, long-ago familiar, that I once knew.

CAPRICCI

Midmorning, the oils mixed, the canal clear and alive with chatter, the painter sits down to his *veduta*. He lays pen and ink beside him in case he needs a quick sketch— quills for the soft lines, metal points for the sharp. It will be a simple scene: the Rialto Bridge spanning the Grand Canal, the Basilica of Vicenza and Palazzo Chiericati on either side. Already the painter can pinpoint what will fall into his view, what will background and sell his work to the English patrons who trek the Grand Tour across the continent to buy his work. He used to be a scenographer after all, a designer of opera sets just like his father. And so those seagulls swarming upon a mess of nets, picking at something not-quite dead, not-quite alive—they must go. Same for the shade cast over the water by that colonnade; he'll scale that back a bit and replace it with light. He has always preferred, in any case, painting sunlight to water. But the dozen or so people peppering the scene, the figures who assume other shapes in the distance—the robed pear standing by the side of the stairs; the gondolier upright like a mantis, punting his extra leg of an oar—these he will keep. These are his drama.

Venice: Caprice View with Palladio's Design for the Rialto Bridge

The tourist would like to take a brief vacation. He would like to see everyone from a different angle. Don't we all need to get away from ourselves sometimes? He looks at the people before him and decides that the robed man next to the bridge's stairs— most likely a priest—resembles not just a pear, but a bell. And that the white-stockinged gentleman in front of the canal has the legs of a crane. But the pose of each—at least this is what it seems—reminds him most of the *conduttori* on the train he took from Rome to Venice. One drearily trudges down the corridor in midnight blue, tapping his fingernails on the seatbacks as he passes; the other crosses his arms in impatience as the tourist fumbles for his ticket, for his admission to scene and city.

The year is 1745, it is unsurprisingly sunny in Venice, and the painter is Giovanni Antonio Canal. He goes by Canaletto, "the little canal," the diminutive given to the painter of water channels and the son of Bernardo (the Big, the Papa, the Grand) Canal. Canaletto paints *vedute*, landscapes and cityscapes, and his large-scale work ranks at the forefront of Venetian *vedutisti*.

James McNeill Whistler would say that "Canaletto could paint a white house against a white cloud." The American so loved the Venetian's level of detail that when he visited the National Gallery in London, he went at once to "*smell* the Canalettos." Pressed to explain his popularity, other critics put it more simply: Canaletto could make the sun shine in his pictures. True, he couldn't do much with water—"chain mail laid over marble," sniped one—but he paid special attention to mortar and stone, the *coto belo chiaro* and *cenerin* of gray-cobbled Venice. And who needed water when one could imagine a sky so uniformly blue that no tint or gild of sun seemed possible? So blue that his early commissions were always delayed until his patrons complained, threatening to leave him for a Piranesi in Rome, and the painter replied with demands for more time, whingeing on about the price of Prussian blue, that essential yet expensive pigment, the one color needed to finish off his masterful, scumbled skies and capture the real thing. Canaletto perfected a type of painting where the central unifier was hidden in broad daylight. He painted sunlight without the sun. He made what was present appear absent.

View of the Piazzetta

The tourist is soaking it in. How the sun shines from everywhere, even in near December! The air smells faintly of sardines but no matter. For there in the distance, a heavy white sail hangs from the boom of a barge—oh how it reminds him of the sheets his mother used to drape over the shower rod. He remembers bunching the heavy wet linens in a corner so the showerhead would not spray them. How wonderful that everything has correspondence and analogy. The tourist is content. Today he will see the Grand Canal; today he will touch Murano glass.

Before he sets to work, Canaletto consults the sketches that came before. He rifles through his papers and runs his hand over the brown ink's crosshatches.

Canaletto is painting a still life, but he's also painting a city. That's one of the difficulties of the *vedutisti*. He must calm the commotion, let it stand as frozen but about to thaw, count the untold steps about to be taken. He is an efficient worker, over 585 paintings in his lifetime, but he must first have everything laid out in front of him. And so what does he do with those figures to his right, the group of men lounging by the wharf, passing back and forth a bottle of white, the sunlight glinting off the glass? Does he keep them or cut them out? What do they discuss so early in the day?

Whatever he decides, he wants his painting to appear timeless. His admirers marvel that Canaletto styled a Venice "closer to the celestial city of Revelation ... pure gold, like unto clear glass." That is, he depicted a city that was not just timeless but at any and all time, a city whose tourists can imagine themselves to be anywhere. Stroll through any first-rate metropolis, his critics say—a Paris, New York, or London—and sooner or later you will round the corner and come upon some aspect of a scene that will remind you so completely, so uncannily, of a Canaletto.

Grand Canal: Looking East from the Campo S. Vio

The tourist is drunk. All that thought about his mother hanging sheets has made him homesick. The corner store—he does not know the name for it, but calls it a bodega—has a chalk sign advertising a liter of wine for three Euros. It is too good to pass up and he has just finished two liters of Nestlé Pure Life. He fills the bottle up with white wine from the keg and finds his friend and they go and sit on a high bench by the Grand Canal. Their legs dangle. They drink the wine quickly because the sun is out and warm white wine has the faint taste of eggs, and he and his friend pretend they are the statues of fish in fountains and try to arc wine from their mouths onto the backs of pigeons that pass beneath their feet.

Those critics must be losing their minds! New York, Paris, London. How can Canaletto's work pass for anywhere but Venice? Start in the 1720s and his paintings sell well enough that Canaletto's name rings as synonymous with his city. When his nephew, the painter Bernardo Bellotto, sold his own work abroad, he signed his canvases with his uncle's name to fetch a higher price. And the art collector William Beckford professed upon visiting Venice, "I have no terms to describe the variety of pillars, of pediments, of mouldings, and cornices . . . that adorn these edifices, of which the pencil of Canaletti conveys so perfect an idea as to render all verbal descriptions superfluous." Canaletto's views became cicerone to his city. Travelers experienced Venice through his eyes and Canaletto through their experience of Venice.

Although, just a moment, please: Do these travelers and tourists see what Canaletto himself saw, or what he wanted them to see? Does it matter?

When it comes down to it, we do not know how he actually viewed his city. We only know how he *thought* his city should be viewed, which is to say how he thought it should be sold.

An Island in the Lagoon with a Gateway and a Church

Once he is drunk and the sun is setting and his friend returns to the hotel to meet the others, the tourist starts to feel romantic and so he ogles the pretty, passing girls. He imagines them aristocrats, the great-granddaughters of the Medici, wanderers of ruined villas. How much like sculpture, how beautiful! The men are not so bad either. On the way back to the hotel, he decides to get lost—a true Venetian experience, his guidebook tells him. Who knows, perhaps he will meet someone from long ago? Anyone, that is, to quell his loneliness, to lend credence to the unreality in which he's washed up.

In 1745, Canaletto is one of only a handful of painters working from direct observation—he gondolas to a certain spot and records what he sees—and so it becomes easy to substitute one of his *vedute* for a view of actual Venice, to assign it documentary accuracy.

But Canaletto also paints capriccios. If his *vedute* were the idealized made realistic, then capriccios were fantasy rendered believable, fiction turned non. Capriccio: a subset of land-and-cityscape painting in which the painter inserts some architectural invention—an archaeological ruin, an imagined assembly of buildings—into the supposed reality of the present-day scene. An alternative way of imagining a city, raw topographic material granted pictorial license. Canaletto believed in the artist's right to modify and redesign facts in the interest of creating a picture. So look again at where we started. The Grand Canal, the Rialto Bridge, the Palazzo, and Basilica? Fantasy. Pure Palladian fantasy. Canaletto is depicting not the actual Rialto, but a never-realized plan to replace the existing structure, a project designed by good old Andrea Palladio, the sixteenth-century architect and classicist. As for the Palazzo Chiericati and Basilica Palladiana, those are landmarks belonging to the city of Vicenza, sixty kilometers to the west.

If by hiding the sun in broad daylight Canaletto made what was present appear absent, then the capriccio, well . . . absence becomes presence. Nostalgia springs magically back into the frame and whimsy forms solid architecture.

Capriccio: A Palladian Design for the Rialto Bridge, with Buildings at Vicenza

The tourist walks around the city and sees what he wants to see. He projects long-lost faces onto anonymous strangers. Often he pauses on his walks along the canal banks, the side streets so narrow and filled with shade, and watches a father rowing his son down the channel.

Canaletto's popularity came at some expense. John Ruskin, that stale old fart, steamrolled him in a diatribe that cemented the painter's reputation for years: "The mannerism of Canaletto is the most degraded that I know in the whole range of art. Professing the most servile and mindless imitation, it imitates nothing but the blackness of the shadows . . . Let it be observed that I find no fault with Canaletto for his want of poetry, of feeling, of artistical thoughtfulness in treatment . . . He professes nothing but coloured daguerreotypeism . . . no virtue except that of dexterous imitation of commonplace light and shade."

Note the points on which Ruskin wants to skewer Canaletto: "mindless imitation," "commonplace light and shade," "daguerreotypeism." As if Canaletto were only aiming—and failing—at documentary photography. As if art and invention belonged to another figure entirely.

Yet what if Ruskin has a point? Take Canaletto out of Venice, and even that dexterous imitation falls apart. The painter moves to London in 1746, and the quality of his work falls so dramatically that the art world accuses him of being an impostor. The public demands he give a painting demonstration to prove he is who he says he is. He so loses his knack for translation—no longer able to make of the English evening the silver and saffron of a Canaletto sunset—that the answer can only be that he's no longer himself.

Though if we speak of the man himself, the hidden unifier, the arranger, we beg the question: who *was* Canaletto actually?

Nighttime Celebration Outside the Church of San Pietro di Castello

The tourist goes to an inexpensive bar with his friends, stands outside, smokes Gauloises, and drinks too many Peronis. The bar's not actually so inexpensive because he forgets to convert his Euros into dollars. He and his friends buy a bottle of limoncello and drink it by the water and try to lift a Smart car from the street onto the curb. They fail. At the hotel, the tourist wanders into a dining room and pees in the corner. He tries to stack a number of wine glasses into a pyramid, but the pyramid falls down, and the glasses break. He sits on a balcony, nursing his cut hand, and kicks his legs out over the street. He didn't expect this, but he is homesick. Two of his friends stand next to him and make out. He falls asleep in the bathtub.

What we know: That he was born in 1697. That his first signed and dated work was a capriccio. That his personality was, according to a Swedish count, "*fantasque, bourru, Baptistise*"— temperamental, abrupt, clownish. That by 1755, Canaletto so tired of London he returned to Venice. That, at the same time, no record of him exists between 1755 and 1760, so that he might not have returned to Venice after all. That Bernardo

Bellotto had good reason for signing his uncle's name on his own work because he painted some of Canaletto's *vedute*. That Canaletto's father painted some as well. That Tiepolo quite possibly painted his figures. That although Whistler said of his paintings "In this work you will find no uncertainty," the public painting demonstration proved very well warranted all the same. That in 1760 a young Englishman and his tutor saw a "little man painting" in a Venetian square. That this little man invited them back to his studio, where he sold them a view of London. That this was most likely Canaletto. That Canaletto wasn't elected to the Venetian Academy until 1763, since a simple landscape painter was considered inferior to history and portrait painters. That when he was elected, he was expected to provide the Academy a painting, but that it took him— *fantasque, bourru, Baptistise*—over three years to submit something. That he submitted a capriccio. That his last signed and dated work ended with the boast: *Anni 68, Cenza Oculi*. Aged sixty-eight, Without Spectacles. That this was 1766. That two years later on April 19, 1768, Canaletto would die at seven in the evening from a fever. That he left behind some old clothes, a few household goods, and twenty-eight small and medium pictures. That his assets were listed as a small property and eighty pounds sterling. That this was not very much for a supposedly prudent bachelor after 585 paintings in a lifetime. That Canaletto never married or had any children. That he had very few friends. That he was, by all accounts, all alone. That the people in his paintings were almost always anonymous. That in his only known self-portrait, he appears as a miniature man in blue, a cow looking over his shoulder as he sits and stares at the viewer, brush in hand, a man so unknown he could be anyone, though he just so happens to be himself.

A View of Walton Bridge

The tourist doesn't really see Venice. Escape becomes cityscape. Fantasy washes over the scene like a coat of pricey Prussian blue.

But the more the tourist looks for others in these scenes, for replacements of the figure lost from his life, the more he realizes he won't find them. Oh why can't these anonymous figures become the face he knows, the face that has left him on his own? The tourist is afraid the only person he'll find is himself. He wants a vacation, but the part of him that wants this is the part of him he wants to forget.

After he saw the capriccio of Palladio's bridge, Basilica, and Palazzo, Aldo Rossi, the twentieth-century Italian architect, wrote that Canaletto created "an *analogous* Venice." He fashioned a scene "as if the painter had reproduced an actual townscape," a city "that we recognize, even though it is a place of purely architectural references."

In other words, Rossi asked a question: it looks like Venice, but why?

For him, Canaletto gave life to an alternative yet functional city, one of "geographical transposition." The capriccio acknowledges the paths a city never takes and so presents a scene that assumes its counterpart's shape—a fantasy to chameleon or ghost itself onto the real, just as Canaletto washed and shaded over his early drafts of a *veduta*.

The realization thrilled Rossi: "I believe I have found in this definition a different sense of history conceived of not simply as fact, but rather as a series of things, of affective objects to be used by the memory or in a design."

A city as a series of the hypothetical, the what-might-have-been. A city as a space for memory to use, to wander, to pick a trail through unspoken words and unchosen paths. Yet also a space for design, a blueprint for future forms. Either way, a fantasy—the reimagined past or posited future—what Rossi called "an analogical representation that could not have been expressed in words."

And so perhaps this lends a bit of credit to those critics who argue that if we walked through a Canaletto, we would be reminded of any city. Not just Venice, but Paris, New York, London. Because really Canaletto does not paint cities. He paints possibilities for them.

Rio dei Mendicanti: Looking South

The tourist wakes up the next morning with a hangover. The Venetian sun! Does it ever stop shining? He looks out the back window and sees laundry hanging on the line. He starts to think of his mother back home alone and his father as well, until he notices that he can't read any of the logos on the drying T-shirts. He checks his contact case and then the trash, but they are both empty, and he blinks many times in quick succession until he feels an itch behind his eyelids. His contacts have done that thing where they travel up into his head. He sighs. He forgot his glasses as well. People will become blurs and he will go the rest of the day hoping the lenses settle back over his eyes so that he can see the sights once again.

If Canaletto created an analogous Venice through its architecture, what did he do for the figures he hatched and cross-hatched? Do they form the texture of an alternative city as well, replete with their own fantasies to play out? Do they trace their own analogous lives out and around the corner of Canaletto's cityscapes?

There is, of course, no real answer to this.

In the painter's early work, the art historian Michael Levey writes that Canaletto treats "people as people." They are "lively and individual, not serving as mere puppets or just providing a garnish to the solid meat of architecture ... His pictures are rich in variety of costume, and even more in variety of action and characters—from boatmen to beggars, via Turks, Jews and priests, servant girls, noblemen, workmen, ladies and children."

But not so in Canaletto's later output. He peoples these with "stereotyped figures" (although what is the above quote, one itches to ask, if not a list of exactly that?) and reduces his characters to components within a composition, as replicable as windows in a facade. One needs imagine only the minute, hair's-width golden ratio spiraled into the background of *Whitehall and the Privy Garden from Richmond House* to realize figures have become deftly placed forms: they are hieroglyphs, a shorthand of blobs and squiggles. Shapes without clear identity. Architecture. In other words, they cater to what people who have never been to one of Canaletto's cities expect to see. Their roles are open, their histories anyone's.

Detail of *Whitehall and the Privy Garden from Richmond House*

The tourist walks to a nearby Laundromat. His friends are still asleep. He wants a place to rest and nods off in a chair by the dryers. When he wakes up, he decides to walk to the station and take the train back to Rome. Without his contacts, he has trouble reading the street signs and can't recognize the buildings he passed last night. It's as if, the tourist thinks, he woke up in another city. He eats McDonald's in the train station. He licks his fingers and walks to the platform but runs into his friends there. They are going for a cappuccino and *cornetto* and convince him to spend another day.

It wasn't just the capriccios. Nearly every one of Canaletto's paintings utilized some degree of invention or underwent some manipulation at his hand. He was the plastic surgeon of eighteenth-century Venice, the nip/tuck of colonnades and piazzas. He hid and rearranged buildings, lengthened and shortened sunlight and shadows as he pleased, blew distance up or dialed it down. He believed, once again, in the "artistic right to modify, move, and rearrange those facts in the interest of creating a picture."

Canaletto painted both what was there and what was better off there, the large-scale logic founded upon the detailed lie. He fashioned the idealized into the believable and won that "old victory of arrangement over accumulation," as Susan Sontag puts it. So that when a critic says that Canaletto "perceive[s] a serene, ordered structure of universal significance"—in a city's fluted columns and arcades or its rows of rounded stone-set windows—that perception implies a good deal of eighteenth-century airbrushing.

A question wiggles its way in here: Isn't there some complicity in all this? Doesn't the viewer, the tourist, the eye desire deception? Don't we want exactly what Canaletto gives us? To be able to forget, to be able to sigh and wish for a place and people that never existed?

Piazza San Marco

The tourist has rallied himself and taken a boat to the Murano islands, walked the arcades at Piazza San Marco, seen the Bridge of Sighs, and stopped in a cybercafé to write two emails. He tries to speak to the waiter at the trattoria where he eats lunch but doesn't know enough of the language to make it past *come vai* and *di dove é*. He takes photographs and decides that when he arrives home again, he will make a gallery of the pictures. In both emails, he uses the phrase "I feel as if I'm seeing the real Venice." The tourist has found in this declaration a different and alternative sense of history.

The painter puts the old drafts away and selects a fresh piece of paper. He stretches, rubs his hands, sips his muddy Venetian coffee. The sun comes out from behind a momentary cloud. And just like that Canaletto begins his sketch, his *scaraboti*, his quick crosshatch and etch. He slides out a drafting compass to help round the basilica's domes, stretches his ruler flat to outline the square. He chalks a few figures on the ground—the blurry bellflower of a doge's robe, the sweep with the flat of a pen to curve a sailor's falling sash.

And then, once this is done, he arranges his oils. He paints from strength to weakness: first the sky, softened to a duller glow; then the buildings, worked up with impasto, layer upon layer of paint to bring sculpture to the canvas; then the water, so viscous and oily that the joke is he discovered pollution before it even had the chance to reach Venice; and finally the figures, those shapely ornaments to dot and fill a plane.

Except, of course, none of this is true. Or rather, the process is true, but the location is just another caprice. Canaletto did make rough sketches on scene, but the chances of his painting out of doors are nothing more than wishful thinking. A misconception spread by Alessandro Marchesini, his first agent, to serve as selling point. Much like the tourist, Canaletto was never actually there. He painted from points of view—fifteen feet above the Grand Canal—that were impossible to inhabit. And so one more thing to add to the list of unknowns: how did he achieve a position that required fantasy to embody? We don't know how he was able to see what he saw (with such detail! with such precision!), much less where he stood to begin with.

The Grand Canal and the Church of the Salute

The tourist takes a train back to Rome that night. His headache is gone. He lies down across his row of seats and bunches his jacket up beneath his head. He puts on his headphones. The *conduttore* makes a squiggle on his ticket and he mouths *grazie*. He closes his eyes and listens to music. The train makes many stops and at each one he opens his eyes and watches a few people file off. Then the train makes a stop and doesn't start again. The lights turn off. He sits up, removes his earbuds. The engine turns off. A car is decabled. He looks around and doesn't see anyone. He runs to the end of the car and peers through the glass, then runs to the other end of the car and does the same. He cups his hands and looks out the window on to his own reflection. Then he moves his head closer and looks out again. He sees black. No one is there.

Canaletto also used (and here Ruskin's cries of "mindless imitation" and "daguerreotypeism" echo briefly) a camera obscura.

It allowed him to frame a scene from multiple perspectives at once, to sketch and sow together a view more expansive than the one offered by reality. Visit his scenes and you will find no single point that encompasses their arrangement of buildings and water.

Although this shouldn't constitute too much of a surprise: Canaletto was once an opera set designer, after all. Flights of fancy constitute the norm.

What if we then thought of Canaletto as trained not so much to insert fantasy into reality, but reality into fantasy? If the capriccio substitutes for the real thing, then does that captured city somehow become more representative of Venice than Venice itself? Is the city that can't be seen—the city that requires some analogy or manufactured perspective to bring it into existence—any less real than the city that can?

And is the person who remains invisible any less real than the person who can be seen, than the anonymous figures the tourist decides to place meaning upon?

Piazza San Marco Looking South and West

The tourist pries open the car doors and walks back along the tracks. He passes solitary, detached cars. He's in a refueling station, but it looks like a train graveyard. He's outside a city, but he's not sure which one. Up ahead a light shines from a single train car. He crosses the tracks and approaches it. Three men in uniform gather there. Two lean against the car's side and the third sits on the steps. The tourist waves and says *Ciao*. The seated man stands up and walks down a step. Then he walks down the rest and stands with the others. The light pools. The tourist sees the men in close-up; he sees their faces as fully as he can see another's face. They look at him and wait. His hands fumble again for his ticket. He realizes he's now at the mercy of another's whimsy. More practically, he realizes that, never having bothered to learn the language, he has no idea how to tell these men who he really is. He realizes he doesn't even know the words to say "I am lost," much less to explain that he never knew where he was to begin with.

But let us end on a high note. *The Stonemason's Yard* is Canaletto at his finest, the perfect balance between his early and more developed styles. The painting bustles with life and the suggestions of the small everyday narratives that take place within the anonymous activities of a city. A small pantsless boy urinates in the foreground. A woman leans out her second-story balcony to whip a sheet through the air. Note how easily the eye is led across the water to the tower of the Carita across the way. Whistler compared this painting to Velásquez; even Ruskin admired it, admitting to a "determined depreciation" of Canaletto on his part.

On the left-hand side of the painting, there's a breadth of alleyway, a slight shiver of light across the water. Here Canaletto "suggests the continuous, unfolding, and ever-alluring experience of the city." He hints at what's just out of sight, the next turn around the corner, the ever-expanding Venice, all the paths the viewer cannot take. One's tempted to use Canaletto as map and compass, to stitch all his views and angles together to form one grand city of analogies, a city in which you can walk around the corner of one scene and into the next. The experiment would fail, of course—we would find ourselves in a city of gaps and lacunae, of hopeless doublings and overlay, an architectural chimera or worse, a Frankenstein as disordered and jumbled and prone to blackout as memory. We must not lose ourselves. That "serene, ordered structure"—one needs to privilege something just to make it back home at the end of the day. We must be content with the limits and edges of Canaletto's paintings and leave those other cities to him. We will abandon him then, to pack up his pens and paper at the end of the day and make his lonely walk back home to the solitude no one knows about, out of the picture, out of Venice, out of Canaletto, somewhere and someone else entirely.

The Stonemason's Yard

There are other times, stumbling around a corner, the afternoon sun nowhere to be seen, a shopping bag of souvenirs from Canal Street clinking against his leg, snowglobes and key chains and a five-by-eight-inch Venetian watercolor, when the bifocals are lifted, the contacts settle back in, and the tourist sees two figures frozen, about to move. There is a space between them as if meant for a small child, as if the hands

are waiting for the child to rush up and grab them. He finds
himself magically again in a Canaletto, a place that exists how
he wants it to exist. He sees, in all its sunlight, a life for the
analogy it might once have been.

THE ROCK SHOP

Roger sets his sixty-four-ounce Polar Pop down on a case of Hohokam axes and says he wants to be preserved in amber when he dies. He throws his head back and shivers his limbs out to mimic a fly. His eyes flutter and neck strains, his expression stuck somewhere between ecstasy and grimace.

Roger mentions how humans have been preserving each other for centuries. The "tar people," murdered bodies found in bogs, kept in tannic acid. Vampires with stakes stuck through their throats. A frozen iceman in Scandinavia discovered with his penis stolen.

Beads of cola sweat down from the rim of Roger's Styrofoam cup. The axe heads are made of stone, willow branches boiled and wrapped around them for the handle, rawhide strapped around that for the grip. A rancher and his sons found them while grazing their cattle. Roger picks up his Pop and describes the kiva houses where the Hohokam held weddings. He leans in. Elders would take peyote and psilocybin, he whispers, and then ceremonially rape the child-bride.

As for the amber, Roger straightens up. "I decided I wanted to look out on all my belongings forever." He gestures around the room, sips his soda, laughs. "Naked," he adds.

The belongings Roger refers to sit twenty miles outside Tucson on Kinney Road, the lonely two-laner where you gas up before hitting the interstate south to Mexico. Nearby is a rifle and pistol range, a saguaro forest, and Old Tucson, a studio town of saloon doors and replica hitching posts that Hollywood built in the 1950s to film Westerns. A big canvas teepee stands in a gravel lot off Kinney where Geronimo's grandson, or so he claimed, held court, charging tourists a dollar to take his picture until the day he was found in the mountains outside Oracle, slumped over in the van he was forbidden to drive since he was over one hundred years old.

Next to this teepee, tucked slightly off the road, you'll find a storefront. Its wood will be weathered the color of root beer, its facade as if built for an Old Tucson shoot and then never taken down.

This is Roger's shop. Rocks of all shapes and sizes fill its yard. Rocks in old wheelbarrows and mine trolleys. Rocks on a foldout table, in baskets and wire mesh cages. Rocks in a shallow ditch with wood trim where a garden was once planned then thought better of. Geodes, two dollars a pound. Banded Onyx, one dollar. A green pickup in the gravel parking lot. On the glass of the store windows, stenciled-out cowboys ride over hills. A sign, handwritten in white paint, says, "We have a large selection of quartz crystals inside." Another: "Proud To Be An American." A third: "Open 9–5, Every Day of the Year."

I first entered Roger's shop three years ago, when my mother flew out to visit me in Tucson. I'd driven past the storefront before she landed and thought this just the place to take her, the woman who never stopped reminding me to send copper and quartz crystal back to her in New York.

When we entered Roger's, we noticed two things. The first: this was the most crowded store we'd ever been inside. The second: it was also the emptiest.

When Renaissance noblemen first displayed their cabinets of wonder, the private collections of natural and artificial curiosities meant to show off their wealth and good taste, they must have had in mind something like Roger's shop. And when these cabinets of wonder grew so copious and cluttered they spilled onto anywhere there was an inch of space—so much so that one prominent eighteenth-century collector, the London architect John Soane, had Pandora's box painted on his ceiling—they paved the way for Roger.

Here is some of what you will find inside Roger's shop: Glass cases of meteorites and tektites, turquoise and wulfenite. A lizard's tracks in shale. Ram's horn. Apache tears. A Mayan penis-piercing tool ("Ouch!" its description reads). Mummi-fied pack rats with gold-plated corpses.

There'll be an Apache hair comb and a forty-five-dollar

pterodactyl tooth. A freeze-dried rattlesnake's head. A wolf's penis bone like a bleached shepherd's crook, glued to a Styrofoam plinth. "Makes an excellent swizzle stick," reads the paper stapled to it. Crucifix nails used in Spartacus's uprising. A sarcophagus carrying the remains of a 4,500-year-old child. A chest-high filing cabinet of alphabetized minerals: chalcopyrite, coal, coke, conglomerate, copper, copper native, copper splash.

You will also find Roger's prized possessions sitting in a glass case: the skull of a Roman gladiator missing his jaw; the skull of a Spanish conquistador killed by the Aztecs; and the skull of a soldier dead at the Alamo, a bullet hole through his occipital, the word *Mexican* inked above it. A picture of a smiling 1950s housewife is taped to the glass case with the caption: "Unattended children will be given espresso and a kitten." Before that, a grainy black-and-white photo of a man being lynched and the words: "All shoplifters will be prosecuted."

What you will not find at Roger's is many people. Grit crunched the floor where we walked. A layer of dust covered the shelves and another layer on top of that. The lights were turned off. You could stroll around, bundle your arms up, and walk out. A house of relics, fittingly, had become a relic itself.

It's said that the difference between a collector and a hoarder is that while a collector takes joy in arranging his accumulations, the hoarder finds none. The collector assembles a museum of the self, but a hoarder still searches for that self. The hoarder holds out an almost perverse hope: the nagging thought that everything, if seen in the right light, contains value.

∞

When he does emerge from his back office, "A Correlated History of the Earth" poster taped to its door, Roger appears in some variation of the following: a blue Route 66 T-shirt, jeans with the cuffs worn away, flip-flops, and a Veterans hat with *U.S.A.* stitched across the brim. A bald eagle perches above the *S*. Its eyes will swivel.

Roger is tall and has a gut. He slouches and his gut sticks out some more. He smells of cigarettes, not necessarily in the sense of someone who's smoked, but of someone who's spent a long time in a house where cigarettes have been smoked. Roger looks telluric. Liver spots pepper his neck and arms and it looks like you could dig a good inch into one of his fingers with a pocketknife and still not draw blood. Burn holes singe his T-shirt, enough to spot a nickel of belly underneath. To say his feet are dirty would not broach their condition. They rival Jesus's in the wilderness.

But what stands out most about Roger is his face. Simply put, it's kind. It's the face of your favorite old, absentminded professor you run into when he's out of quarters at the coin laundry. Roger smiles when you find something you like—a puddingstone from the Great Lakes, a concretion like flattened cow dung—and explains its geology to you. Then he wraps it up in paper towels and hands it to you for free. He exudes that treasured quality of making you feel like a kid again, of letting you know—even if you don't know him at all—that everything is all right. If you protest and offer to pay, he'll say what really matters is not the exchange of money but the exchange of information, that with each item he gives away he also offers up a piece of himself.

At the counter, Roger explained to me and my mother that he and his brother Rick inherited the property after their parents died. The brothers were born on Long Island after World War II. Roger studied paleontology at the University of New Mexico, then worked at New York's Museum of Natural History and the Arizona-Sonoran Desert Museum, Tucson's open-air wildlife habitat a few miles down Kinney Road. At one point, in the mid-1990s, he led a team of paleontologists that discovered the bones of a new dinosaur in the nearby desert. They christened it the Sonorasaurus.

Rick, Roger's brother, is missing his middle and ring fingers on his right hand. He tells his Boy Scout troops that a bear ate them, but really he lost them in different work accidents. The mummified pack rats are his handiwork. He finds them dead in his backyard, hangs them up on a clothesline, then dips them in a barrel of gold before spray-painting on a final coat. A framed picture of Roger and Rick from the 1985 Tucson Winter Skeet Shooting League—the brothers nearly identical in trucker hats, mustaches, and heft—hangs on the wall next to the back room.

Roger seems to disdain making any profit; instead, he gives what he calls "deals." When my mother and I dumped our haul at the register—copper, quartz, a mummified pack rat, and the cowboy belt buckle given away for free on any purchase over fifteen dollars—Roger ambled over, waved a hand,

and quoted a price much lower than it should have been. A few years ago, he said, he even gave away most of his stuff. "You did?" my mother asked, taking a look around. "Doesn't look like it." "Oh yeah," Roger said. "I have loads more. I even have a mummy out back." He folded his hands on the table. "You wanna see?"

Roger led us through his backyard—caliche, cacti, little shade—to a low-slung, one-story house. We entered a screened-in porch. Laundry piled in front of the washing machine. Plastic soda bottles and old DVDs carpeted the floor. Empty packs of Marlboro Lights scattered across a glass table.

Roger's living room was a menagerie. A severed elephant's foot, stretched into a bowl, sat on a side table. "I clip its toenails," Roger told us. A green-glazed turtle rested on a buffet. "Oh, I love this," my mother exclaimed and asked how much it cost. Roger told her it was his fifth-grade pottery project. In the corner, a snake hid in a glass terrarium, its skin shed onto wood chips. The hide of a platypus hung on the wall. "It's the only mammal that injects venom," Roger said. He pointed out the fourth toenail that hooked into its victim's flesh. A small statue of Horus, the Egyptian falcon god, stood next to the elephant's foot.

In the far corner of the living room, next to the bedroom hallway, stood an Egyptian mummy. Roger had propped its sarcophagus upright and cut out a square of wood to display the skull. A clip-on reading light attached to the wood. "I only did the one sacrilegious thing," he said by way of explanation. "Otherwise, I think this is as good a home as any."

The mummy, Roger said, belonged to a sixteenth-dynasty pharaoh. He was missing an arm, lost in battle to the Hittites. Roger speculated a chariot might have lopped it off. "This guy was a brave one. He was probably leading the charge."

Upright, it stood shorter than you might expect. I had never seen one in person and what I anticipated—first-aid gauze, a solid cast between body and casing—wasn't there. There seemed little telling what was packaging and what skin.

Inherited seems the wrong word, so let's say Roger came into the pharaoh when he worked at the Museum of Natural History. He befriended an old Egyptologist, whose house he visited for tea. When the Egyptologist died, he left Roger the mummy. Roger and Rick hoisted it onto a dolly, wheeled it down the Egyptologist's stairs, and eventually—this explanation of its shipment is elided—ended up with it in Tucson. "I don't focus too much on whether this was legal," Roger said. He named the mummy Heck. It's lived with him ever since.

Roger brushed his fingers over the hieroglyphs running down the sarcophagus. "Extrapolating," he said, pointing to the uppermost, "this refers to the pharaoh's name." For the next one, "This is his name in the afterlife." And the third, "This means that if you open the tomb, you're cursed and will die."

I raised my eyebrows. Did he believe any of this? I had asked the same thing about the magical healing properties listed in his descriptions of Sedona vortex rocks and Roger had given the same answer: "I think it becomes true if you want it to be true." Roger rubbed the mummy's head and asked if I wanted to as well. "Come on, it's for good luck." "Are you nuts?" my mother yelled, to which of us I couldn't tell. I reached toward the head—it seemed, perhaps perversely, the polite thing to do—and gave a hesitant pat. "Tom!" she punched my arm. The skull was smooth and cold. It felt very brown. I looked at my palm to see if any had rubbed off.

My mother objected because we are a superstitious family—years of watching the Mets on television and thinking our actions could affect faraway and seemingly unrelated circumstances. If we willed it in our heads and then enacted it through some bodily motion, it would come true. I'd sit cross-legged, counting to four in my head, rubbing my palms together in a steady counterclockwise. My father would rock back and forth in his chair, holding his empty bowl of pasta. My mother sat in my father's green armchair, her feet propped up on the footstool, back rigid with her arms extended straight out, holding a stretch and making a *Zzzz* sound through her teeth as if shooting electricity out of her fingertips and into the television set. This way, whatever action she wanted to take place—a wild pitch, a walk, a hitta homer hitta homer hitta homer—would come to pass. When it worked, we all claimed credit. When it didn't, then it was someone else's fault.

Before we left Roger's house, the three of us stopped in the hallway. Roger told us his dad had bought the property to turn it into a working gold mine. Really, Roger said, he thought this was where his father brought his girlfriends. He winked. He and Rick had to take their mother's name because their father's was too well-known.

"What did your father do?" my mother asked.

"He was a film director." My mother scanned the black-and-white photos in the hall. She nudged me to look at one: an older man at a party in a tuxedo, tall, bald, blue-eyed like Roger.

"What was his name?" she asked.

"Otto Preminger," Roger said.

I should mention, before proceeding any further, that alongside my affection for Roger and his shop, there creeps a doubt. The cabinet is a bit too curious. It's not every day I walk into a store in the middle of the Sonoran desert selling gladiators' skulls and indigenous Australian pointing bone necklaces. Nor do I visit many places that so strenuously insist on the legality and "100 percent authenticity" of everything for sale. If you have to try so hard to prove it, I think, then what do you have to hide?

Take, for example, Roger's descriptions. Here's what he writes for the pointing bone necklace: "This artifact has actually killed people. The act of boning someone is always done in secret, attended by a small number of suitably initiated men, who act as witnesses and support the 'sorcerer' in a low chanted ceremony where the bone is pointed in the direction of the victim and through 'diabological agency' draws a little blood (or life essence through the air) to the bone."

This baffles me. Does Roger expect others to believe this, or is he only fulfilling his journalistic duties? Why use the words "actually killed people" instead of "supposedly"? Given what's written, it's unclear if Roger the collector believes in the power of his collection or if he feels these beliefs are worth naming because they are a part of their objects, however unreal.

Most of all, there's the problem of spelling. Call me fussy, but here is Roger's description of a Roman crucifixion nail:

$49 100% guaranteed, as described
ANCIENT ROMAN IRON
CRUCIFIXION NAIL
c.a. 2,300 years old ound in mass
exicution grave, ner Brundisium on the
Adriatic coast of Italy on the "Apian
Way" where 6000 crucifixes took
place around 312 BC. More below line

These typos appear everywhere. Wouldn't one expect a paleontologist and historian to have care when spelling "found," "near," "execution," or "Appian?" Why wouldn't the detail used to assert the accuracy and legitimacy of the objects extend to the language used to present them?

Of course, my skepticism in the shop might also be my hope. What could be more interesting than if Roger were faking it all, creating a false self and passing it off as the real thing, "100 percent guaranteed as described"?

Pyrite, which Roger sells in spades, is more colloquially known as fool's gold. It's false, in the sense that it leads someone to make a mistake and overvalue a lesser substance. But the iron pyrite in Roger's shop is priced higher than the nuggets of real gold—which is to say that one's left to question whether real value lies with authenticity or its false luster.

Otto Preminger, the famed Austrian American film director responsible for *Laura* and *Anatomy of a Murder*, had, to put it lightly, a notorious streak in Hollywood. Like many directors, his temper created headlines. He was known alternatively as "The Terrible-Tempered Mr. Preminger," "the most hated man in Hollywood," and the caustic "Otto the Sweet." He bucked many of the protocols established by the House Un-American Activities Committee, casting an openly gay actor, Clifton Webb, in 1944's *Laura*, and depicting rape and sexual assault in a manner (those courtroom panties) never before seen in *Anatomy of a Murder*. But Preminger might have been best known for his affairs: Dorothy Dandridge, the African American actress in *Carmen Jones*, and Gypsy Rose Lee, the burlesque performer who gave birth to Erik Preminger, Otto's illegitimate but eventually acknowledged son.

Whether or not Preminger had other extramarital children, whether any of them were Roger or Rick, or whether this is Roger's own paternal longing—I have no idea. He had a boy and a girl with his third wife, Hope Bryce, but no other children on the record, and when I email Foster Hirsch, Preminger's definitive biographer, he says he ran across no such name as Roger's in his research. Preminger did live some of the time in New York City, close to Roger and Rick's birthplace. And he might very well have been familiar with Old Tucson

Studios and the surrounding landscape, putting him in a position to buy the property.

But Pima County records show a Helen and Peter with Roger's last name as the original owners of the land where Tucson Mineral and Gem World now stands and the store as built in 1976 before being willed to Roger and Rick. Helen, who would have been Roger's mother, was born September 26, 1919, in Long Island, New York, and died in December of 2005. Peter died in 2003 and was an editor on a few films. Perhaps Preminger met Helen through Peter. But who else could Peter be but Helen's husband since he was born only two months after Helen in 1919 and in Connecticut no less?

The results do not substantiate Roger's claims. Nor do they entirely rule them out. The same applies to when Roger mentioned offhandedly, as we shuffled from his house back to his shop, that a few weeks ago he and Richard Gere grabbed breakfast at the diner across the road. The actor and his father, Roger said, had been old friends.

But if this is false or less-than-reliable information, then suspicion must vein through everything else: Roger's deciphering of the mummy's hieroglyphs, the information listed and misspelled, the relics and artifacts, and ultimately Roger himself—his identity, his authenticity, his livelihood, his life. Not to mention, say, his assurance that no such bad luck will befall you if you rub a mummy's head.

A collector displays a self and a hoarder searches for one. Perhaps what matters most, however, isn't which self one is—hoarder or collector, pack rat or curator—but what that self requires of its objects.

Most of Roger's possessions come from people not his own. Many come from civilizations and cultures that Roger or people like Roger and myself have helped to expel from their ancestral home—the American Indian museum Roger stocks up at when it shuts down, the ranchers who find others' relics on their land, the cotton farm Roger buys so he can piece together its Navajo pottery.

If a collection memorializes its collector, then I wonder what comes at the expense of that memory. Ruins and artifacts may cement the id of a collector, but they also preserve the work done by lost civilizations. Heck's reading light, the Mayan penis-piercing tool ("Ouch!"), the wolf penis bone ("an excellent swizzle stick")—what hay should be made of Roger's treating these objects as a joke or, worse yet, trophies? Just what does a curiosity cabinet make curious?

All around us—the stunt teepee where Geronimo's grandson sat; the Old Tucson studios with their cowboy-and-Indian facades; I-10, Nogales, and its wall an hour away—is evidence of the often-violent and always irremediable change wrought upon a land in the creation of a new identity. The evidence of the somewhat surreal lengths people who think they own that land will travel to in order to wrap up and preserve that identity, to dip it in gold and say here it is, shiny and plated, ready to last, and if you spend fifteen dollars, there's a free tin star and a cowboy belt buckle in it for you.

What is the right way to treat the relics that do not belong to you, but in some way define you? How should we treat our subject matter—what we study and collect and try to piece together—whether we believe its truth or not? I should ask Roger this, but maybe I should also ask myself.

After my mother, I would visit Roger's shop with my girlfriend Sarah. For three years, we would drive out when we lived in Tucson and then, after we moved away, we would come back and visit. Roger liked Sarah; he strung a peridot-pendant necklace together for her on her birthday and answered her questions before he did mine.

Then one day I typed Roger's name into a search engine and clicked on his Facebook profile. Here is what I found:

A split-image of baboons piled on top of a car and young black men on a police cruiser in the Baltimore riots following Freddie Gray's death. "See any difference?" Roger writes.

A photoshopped image of three chimpanzees wearing clothes and below, Roger's caption: "On Russia's 2016 Moscow University calendar, they show what might be an average appearing family unity in a liberal Western nation with an open door immigration policy."

Another post that begins: "Slavery ain't entirely what you thought it was..."

On December 6, 2015, the post: "Did all these men and women die for THIS?????? if you voted for this Islamist shame on you! If you voted for this traitor you're his comrade in arms and you've spit on the graves of every man and woman who died defending America so that someone like Hussein Obama could never hold ANY public (or private) office."

And a few weeks earlier, on November 19, 2015, this: "I believe there's a more formal name for climate change...Winter, Spring, Summer & Fall...I've read about global warming seriously ever since scientists and divisors developed this scam because there is so much money for them to be maid by supporting the lie."

At first, I thought I had clicked on the wrong profile. "I just can't believe that's the same guy," my mother said when I told her. "That's not the man I met." But then I saw a picture of Roger next to three women in bikinis in Times Square ("No John, these weren't trannys. I know boobs when I see them...."), and I recognized the same fervency of description, the misspelled and oddly capitalized words, the periods and punctuation marks marching to their own beat. Facebook too, of course, can be its own cabinet of wonder: it collects the private self and puts it on public display. I remembered Roger's rape jokes and penis jokes and the skull with the word *Mexican* inked above its bullet hole, the black-and-white photo of a lynched, possibly Hispanic man taped to the glass case. I thought maybe this was the real self in front of me the entire time, the one I had avoided seeing. Maybe I had convinced myself of Roger's maxim as well: *it's true if you want to believe it's true.*

I felt sad. I had so much wanted to trust Roger. The story of his father. His explaining, with great delicacy, the anioncation ratio of gold-plating mummified pack rats. Or his telling of how concretions formed in the Great Lakes over tens of thousands of years ago, that they start from a very small nucleus and then grow layer upon concentric layer into a shape that represents what time collects but also distills. I had hoped that someday a visitor would make the hairpin turn over Gates Pass, drive through the saguaro forest, and turn left on Kinney to find Roger and myself, the collection and collector, suspended in our amber, expressions mid-yowl, a sign under us saying "kills just by pointing at you," or "100 percent guaranteed as described," or simply "Ouch!"

And all he turned out to be was a mean old man, stoking his quiet bigotry in his cluttered office so as to putter out and kindly answer questions.

Sarah and I visited Roger one last time after we found his Facebook page. We went back to Tucson for a wedding and decided to drive out.

When we entered the store, we found a teenage girl working the register. It was the first time we'd seen someone else there besides Roger or Rick. She was the daughter of Roger's friend. A security alarm blared whenever the door opened and, behind the register, a video camera fed tape to the office. It was the summer of the presidential election. Roger shuffled out in a black T-shirt and dirty flip-flops. He recognized Sarah before he recognized me. It was almost her birthday again.

We were polite to Roger just as he was polite to us. He showed us his latest purchase, the femur and tibia of a Mexican soldier, an arrowhead sticking out of it at a comically straight angle. His skulls were missing. Afterward, we learned they'd been stolen. When the local news interviewed him, Roger said the thieves must be "devil worshippers." On Facebook, he wrote, "I'd like to nail them to the wall." The skulls had been there over fifty years. Their descriptions were still taped to the glass shelf.

After a little while, Sarah asked Roger about a crystal pendulum she had noticed. He told her to open her palm. He swung the pendulum above it, and then he placed it in her free hand. He said she must hold it over her palm until it made only the slightest quiver. She must think of a question, a yes or no question of great importance, but one whose answer she did not yet know. If the crystal swung clockwise, then the answer was yes. Counterclockwise, no.

Sarah asked Roger the ever-logical question: did he believe in this? Roger paused, as he always did, and wet his lips. He said the pendulum's answers were just a reflection of our mind. That the brain subconsciously knows its answer and delivers that information to our body. He said God is not some guy sitting on a throne decreeing this or that, but all the forces and laws of the universe of which we only know a fraction. That this is more divine than anything conjured by the vision of a man.

I thought of all the questions I would ask if Roger had given the pendulum to me. I searched for the right one. Collections are mayhem. We make meaning of them in so many ways. The only conclusion I could draw was the obvious one: that Roger, like God, wasn't one or the other but all of these things. An old man in front of you in a T-shirt and flip-flops is both kind and racist, generous and bigoted, hatred and love. What would I admit if I said my fondness for him outweighed my knowledge, that I still believed the fraction I saw in front of me? What did it matter if he was telling the truth if the meanings we made said more about us than the person we made them about?

I looked back at the pendulum. Sarah had steadied it. She thought of her question. Slowly, it began to swing.

When it had stopped, Roger said very quietly, "Good. Now drop it in your hand. Gently. Feel it? There, it's yours." And he took her hand in his and closed it around the answer.

PARALLAX

First, disable the smoke alarm. Then look for rooftop tar, printer ink, the chunk of asphalt you pocket where the road is torn up. Drop a measure of this on a surface set to sear. A frying pan will do. Petroleum, black and viscous, will begin to smoke. Clouds rise and disperse in strange shapes. Give them a few fans. Keep track of their patterns on the air. Simple as that, you are looking at sunspots.

Well, not sunspots per se, but only their imitations, at earthly materials emulous of the celestial. At what Galileo Galilei likened them to in his *Letters on Sunspots*. He suggested using the bitumen found in tar or asphalt to approximate their shapes, in the same paragraph where he went on to write, "I do not mean to assert anything positively . . . I do not wish to mix dubious things with those which are definite and certain."

What Galileo believed definite and certain about sunspots was this: they were contiguous to the sun's surface, they generated and decayed like clouds, and they were extremely large, though not so large as Venus. He believed it vain to determine their true substance. That it's sometimes easier to explain what's farther away than what rests close at hand.

A sunspot also grows on one's skin, a blemish the result of overexposure to the sun. My father, born in Brazil with Swiss skin, developed a number of these cancers, basal cell carcinomas to be harvested out. He'd come home after a visit to the dermatologist with a butterfly Band-Aid on his nose, a small sealed thumbprint on his forehead. Once he showed up with his ear bandaged, the tip snipped off, like a dog that had been caught in a fight.

I have my father's skin, the skin that one day turns us into lizards. But I see no signs yet of the inherited trait, just a few white freckles, a loss in pigmentation. Like the sun's, mine are mere blemishes, harmless if cared for. The most they do is signal that the body they rest upon moves in time and space. That it will one day burn up and disappear.

From June 2 to July 8 in 1612, Galileo recorded sunspots. He drew these to corroborate his arguments in *Letters on Sunspots* and refute those made by Christoph Scheiner, who had observed them in Augsburg the year before. Scheiner, a Jesuit astronomer, wished to retain the heavens' perfection and so hypothesized that the spots were distant from the sun, satellites or small planets passing between it and the earth, momentarily darkened by its brightness. In concluding that the spots existed on the sun's surface, Galileo placed imperfections upon what was believed perfect.

He also concluded that the sun itself moved, rotating from west to east around its own center every twenty-five days. It would take a dozen or so days for a sunspot to pass from view and a dozen more for its return. Galileo believed the spots to reappear, but because they continued to expand and condense when out of sight, he could not be sure that what had vanished had now returned.

Galileo also misjudged size. Sunspots are immense: an average spot swallows up both Venus and Earth. A monstrosity approximates Jupiter.

In my childhood home, my parents built a solar system to hang from my ceiling. They cut planets out of wood, looped thread through their tops, and hung them from quarter-inch hooks. The sun in the corner, then the planets in order. They fashioned Saturn's rings out of wire, used cotton balls for Earth's clouds, sprinkled glitter on the wooden circles to indicate the surrounding stars. I stared up at these as an infant, my father and mother on either side of the crib, reciting the names as if trying to orient me on a vast scale. It worked so well my mother claims my first word was *Jupitah*. An unlikely story, yet only she remains with the authority to tell it. We moved out of that first apartment, and my parents packed the solar system and hung it from their new bedroom. It stayed there for many years before my mother stripped it down and threw the planets into storage.

To disprove Scheiner's claim that sunspots were separate planets, Galileo used parallax: the effect created when the position of an object appears to differ based on where it's viewed. Simply put, we see things differently from different places. If the spots were planets moving between the sun and Earth, they would appear outside of the solar disk at some point during the earth's orbit. But Galileo observed that spots fell within the same narrow zone of the sun. Not only that, no matter where on Earth people observed the spots, they fell within the same arrangement. What Galileo telescoped in Florence, Daniello Antonini saw in Brussels and Lodovico Cigoli in Rome. The spots could be drawn from anywhere. They resisted parallax.

There are specific types of parallax rooted in our physical limits. Geocentric parallax, when celestial bodies become displaced because we observe them from the earth's surface and not its center. Heliocentric parallax, because we observe them from the earth and not the sun.

There is another parallax, not a displacement of bodies but disembodiment itself. The parallax that came when my father and I walked across the park to his work and he led me to the microscope at his desk and I pressed the eyepiece to my socket until it left a red mark. Those eukaryotes, floating and dividing, quivering on their jellied stage. When something becomes disembodied, we struggle to see it for what it really is. When someone becomes disembodied, we struggle to see him for what he once was.

My mother took down the mobile because she developed what she terms *cosmophobia*. It's exactly what it sounds like: a fear of the universe, specifically the night sky, its stars and its moon.

I thought it was a joke at first. She'd tell people she had just met, "I have cosmophobia."

"What's that?" they'd ask.

"I hate the sky!" she'd say.

When she takes the poodle out for his nightly walk at her house in the country, she keeps her eyes on the road. If the moon hangs low and she catches sight of it, she'll shudder. If I'm out with her, I'll point out the constellations I see and remark how beautiful they look. "Stop it, stop it!" she'll scream, and then she'll tell the dog, "Don't listen to him," before scooping him up and taking him inside. I am joking and she is joking but we are also, of course, not.

Letters on Sunspots did not overhaul the geocentric organization of the heavens, but it did point to a system that would. At the end of his last letter, Galileo endorsed Copernicus, foreseeing his system's "universal revelation" with "little fear of clouds or crosswinds." Though this was not the exact case (and though he would later refute this), Galileo took a step he could not take back. He dragged Scheiner with him, in thrall to his orbit like one of Jupiter's moons.

One can't help but feel sorry for the Jesuit. What do we do with the news that shatters our hypotheses, the revelation which forces us to rebuild a world? Or the realization that the world has always been built this way, but that only now—because you've swung around on the globe and drifted in latitude—it appears as such. I imagine Scheiner must have felt the way we do when a loved one betrays us. Or the way we do when a loved one dies, which is its own sort of betrayal, because that is not supposed to happen to us, at least not so soon.

In her enamel class at the YMCA, my mother makes copper clocks. For a long time, even after my father's death, she made universe clocks, in which the second and hour hands moved over a glazed indigo background (the night sky) and small multicolored baubles (the stars and planets). She made many of these, handing them out as Christmas and birthday presents. It's a funny idea—keeping time out of what seems beyond it. But cosmophobia hit and now she makes clocks with sheep in the background. The universe became a former friend, one that offered to take care of someone for her and then double-crossed her. It swallowed that something up without even the sense to apologize or admit mistake, and now she has cut off conversation, avoids eye contact when they run into each other on the street. She loves the sheep on her clocks because they resemble the ones that graze on the hillside opposite her window in the country. But these clocks conceal no secrets: in the end, she's counting sheep.

In the year 807 CE in France, Charlemagne ruled as Holy Roman Emperor, people dressed in sack-like tunics, and a black smudge passed over the face of the sun for eight straight days. Clouds obscured the dark spot's entrance and exit, but it looked for all the world like the passage of Mercury.

Yet it wasn't. It could not have been, Galileo argued, because that planet travels so quickly it can't reside within the sun's sphere for seven hours, much less eight days. The smudge must have been a sunspot.

There was, of course, no way to know this if you were alive in 807 CE. No way to build your own telescope, as Galileo did in 1609, because the Dutch had not yet invented it. Though this wouldn't mean you were alone. We've been interpreting and misinterpreting sunspots for centuries, choosing to see them as we please. We've cured and salted their mystery, preserved them against their own heat, and taken from their smoke the signals we need to survive.

My mother and I are not joking those nights in the country because I want her to accept what she refuses and she wants me to accept her refusal. It's ridiculous, this game of chicken, this incessant pointing at the moon. Perhaps just as ridiculous as being asked to continue a life where what gave that life meaning has been removed. If my father is absent, then she believes she can will that other system, the universe that confirms his absence, to disappear as well.

In her cosmophobia, my mother has moved closer to the sun. "I love the sun," she tells me over the phone. "It's ours. He makes things grow. It's responsible for life."

"Did you call it a he?" I ask.

"I call it an it. *S-u-n* not *s-o-n*. Don't get ahead of yourself," she says.

"Do you like the earth?" I ask.

"I like the earth. I love the grass, the trees, the birds. The sheep." She goes on, but then another voice obscures hers—the phone lines have become mixed up and I must wait through this snippet of conversation until her voice returns. When it does, she is asking me where I am.

"I'm here," I say and ask again: "Do you ever think the sun is one of those stars that has already died and we just don't know it yet?"

"Tom," she pauses, "we would know it. It takes nine seconds for its light to reach us. It's only ninety-three million miles away."

"What about sunspots?"

"Oh, I love sunspots," she gushes. "They're the ones that fuck up all our technology."

Sunspots are neither blemishes nor smokes, but areas of intense magnetism on the sun's surface. This magnetism leads to another definition: sunspots as a notional cause of an odd error. Why did the television screen suddenly go blank? Sunspots. What caused this unforeseen and disastrous event, this irrevocable loss? Sunspots. If we don't fully understand something, we attribute unknown causes. Sunspots have been blamed for the Great Depression and climate change. Their frequency affects the amount of ions in the air, so we say they alter our moods. Their magnetic storms disrupt radio communications and interfere with electronics or, in my mother's words, fuck up all our technology. The voice that crackles through the telephone wire while I speak with my mother. Is it a ghost? Is it my father? No, sunspots.

My mother did once contemplate the universe. Scorpius RA 17h 57m 40s D −37° 33' is a star in the Milky Way. After my father died, my mother contacted the International Star Registry and paid to rename this star *Rafael, Judy, and Tommy*. The dedication was retroactive to the day of his death, as if that were when the three of us packed up the wooden planets and relocated once more, shooting forth from Earth to star. The International Star Registry has no official authority with which to redesignate celestial bodies (they're really something of a swindle), but that is all well and good because my mother now prefers to forget there's a ball of gas out there with our names on it. The dedicatory plaque hangs in a corner of my room. I ask her how she can love the sun and hate the stars when the sun too is a star, when stars, if seen from a different perspective, could also be suns. "But it's *our* sun," she says.

"Those other ones are far away and probably dead. All they do is twinkle. I don't give a shit about twinkling."

The star my mother chose fell in the Scorpius constellation because that is my astrological sign. This made sense in terms of the celestial narrative she had constructed, if she or I were to see a son as the continuation of a father's story. If we believed that the spot the sun's rotation carries away from us will return—altered, transformed, and perhaps unidentifiable, but still in some essence the same. Most of us, I think, would like to assign stories to the stars. Galileo cast astrological charts for his patrons and pupils to earn some extra money on the side. He even cast them for his daughters.

According to Galileo, he and Scheiner shared at least one point in common: both believed sunspots were "not lakes or caverns in the body of the sun." Here's another: they were both wrong.

"As a matter of fact that is precisely what sunspots are," Stillman Drake, Galileo's translator, writes in a footnote. In 1769, Alexander Wilson, the Scottish astronomer, concluded that sunspots were actually saucer-shaped depressions in the star's photosphere. As if caught in a vortex, hydrogen sweeps into one's center and forms a hurricane on the sun's surface. Which is to say: we look at sunspots and see not a blemish or an imperfection, but a hole that can't be filled.

∞

If our fundamental system is upended, if our father or husband suddenly dies and we realize that the cosmos do not remember but forget us, then we either reject the new system offered or we force our own interpretation. Sunspots become not magnetic storms in the photosphere, but magical planets that circle the sun, invisible then darkly illuminated. They return and we once again feel the pleasant hum, the throb of a completed cycle. My mother rejects, but I tint my telescope with a rose-hued lens, like Scheiner used to do, so that the reality I should by now be familiar with appears novel and reasonable. I seek out parallax.

Although his letters were in response to Scheiner's, Galileo did not address them to him. In fact, Galileo did not know whose arguments he responded to: Scheiner wished to remain anonymous and so signed his letters with a pseudonym. He called himself *Apelles latens post tabulam*—Apelles behind the curtain—honoring the apocryphal story of the Greek painter who hid behind one of his paintings to hear what criticisms people offered. What's more, Apelles and Galileo did not exchange letters directly but sent them through an intermediary named Marc Welser, who, like Galileo, was a member of the Lyncean Academy. Apelles wrote in Latin, but Galileo wrote in Italian, a language his counterpart did not speak. Apelles would have to wait for Welser to translate the letter before he could respond. Galileo only knew that Apelles was a Jesuit, did not speak Italian, and believed the sun to be a perfect entity. Both men, however, were similar in one respect: they could not address the you they were really talking to.

∞

Welser wrote Galileo that he received his letters "like manna from heaven," a funny if stock turn of phrase to apply to one who'd find himself contradicting the Church. Yet what caused Galileo such trouble was not the content of what he said as much as the position from which he presented it. It was another case of parallax. The Church insisted that Galileo label his work *istoria* instead of *dimostrazione*. The words are cognates: in order to continue writing, he would have to transform the scientific into the storied, demonstrable proof into fancy.

My mother waits for her grass to grow and the sheep on the hillside to eat it. I project my father outward. I imagine one day a sunspot will form and release a solar flare, within which, bound up with all those megatons of TNT, he'll exist in some part. The eruption will hurl him outward, like slingshot or cannon blast, and he will become matter in space, waiting for me to reach him before he grows cold. I must fling myself out there as well. And I feel sometimes, briefly and wonderfully, as if I could.

But for now, like Galileo and Apelles, I too cannot reach the you I truly want to reach. I do not know how to address this you—what pseudonym you now go by, what painting you hide behind—just as I do not know if you would recognize my attempt. I do not even know if we still speak the same language, if I need another you to translate this, a starry messenger to crackle through the line and relay these words.

∞

I go to a planetarium to see sunspots. It's noon and bright. "We project them onto a flat white surface," the girl at the desk tells me. I walk in to find a round table, the size and height of my kitchen table. Ten feet above it, a mirror juts out from the wall. A semicircle of light hits the mirror and travels upward to a second larger mirror. The second mirror, angled downward, refracts a crescent of sunlight. Within the table's circle, a square of light is inscribed—the mirror's reflection—and at the square's edge, a sliver of brighter light, no bigger than my lunula. It's sunlight. I look down, ready to trace.

But there are no little black spots. The circle is empty, jellied, lifeless like the slide of a microscope before the petri dish slips underneath. The light quivers as if afraid to draw breath. I gaze back up at the circle on the wall and then I look around the sealed room, its artificial lights, its security cameras that look briefly like telescopes. I realize there is still mystery here, still illusion based on what position I stand in. I look back at the brick wall. There are no sunspots, but there's something else—there is sunlight itself.

The light comes from a skylight across the planetarium. The skylight is cut into the ceiling, difficult to spot unless you stand directly below it. I walk underneath, next to a hollow plastic asteroid where a boy and his father watch a video. The boy looks at me, puzzled that I'm standing so close.

The light hits a mirror that hangs from the skylight and

the mirror bounces the light to another, mounted on the wall like a large magnifying glass. This mirror projects the light thirty feet across the room onto the brick wall. I walk back to the flat white table. The sliver of light hovers and shakes and grows smaller. It's like watching the sun set when you can actually see the sun move and it looks like it sets inch by inch but really it does not, when that is just a result of your being on Earth and not seeing it from its true celestial angle, when really there is so much more to the sun than that, but all the same it looks small and a few seconds later when it disappears, it looks dead, it looks gone.

THE ETERNAL COMEBACK

The most secure underground vault in the world sits 650 feet below the earth's surface in an old salt mine outside the town of Hutchinson, Kansas. Inside: over thirty-five football fields worth of storage space, encased in a four-hundred-foot-thick salt formation that can withstand a nuclear blast. The vault is advertised as the world's largest time capsule. Its motto: *For Security, Forever.*

Somewhere within the vault's 1.7 million square feet sit a hundred or so boxes, each the size of a ream of printer paper. The contents of these boxes are precious, known only to the people who assembled them. In 150 to 200 years, these people will unearth their boxes, unpack and inspect each one, and then, depending on the individual, perhaps clutch the contents to his or her chest and weep. In some cases, these boxes will save lives: they may turn these people into people again. For what makes each box so cherished—so much so that it's buried forty-five stories underground in a Cold War–era vault built to withstand all kinds of earthly apocalypse—is that those who first packed the boxes at the beginning of the twenty-first century will be the same ones to unpack them hundreds of years later.

At least, if all goes according to plan.

Bree and I were already sweating. Headed north on Arizona's I-10 early on a late September morning, we were making the two-hour drive from Tucson to Scottsdale to visit the Alcor Life Extension Foundation. At nearly 1,000 members and 127 patients and counting, Alcor is the largest cryonics institute in the world and the name most commonly associated with the cryonics movement, the preservation of bodies at exceedingly low temperatures in the hopes that future technology restores them to life. Ted Williams's head sits inside Alcor's facilities; Simon Cowell and Larry King plan to end up there as well. As much as cryonics has a past or, rather, a future, it is Alcor.

The Toyota's AC kicked on in sporadic blasts and the air pulsed with heat. I'd put the same late Bob Dylan album on loop to kick us into the proper morbid mood. The two of us had yet to shower. Bree, a friend from grad school, offered me a stick of gum and texted her girlfriend, Lela, on our progress. Alcor's free public tour started at 10 a.m. and we were both a little jittery at the prospect, unsure of how to behave in the face of something we didn't believe. Would we pretend to be prospective members in spite of our baby faces? Sign up for storage boxes in the underground vault in Hutchinson, Kansas, as other Alcor members had done? Or would we tell them that Bree, a poet, scrapped preparation for her afternoon class and came along only to indulge a nostalgia for *Futurama*, the show in which the lead character is accidentally cryonically frozen for a thousand years?

Taking the tour seriously, we agreed, was difficult. Cryonics was creepy and, in some respects, terrifying. But we wanted to discover just what exactly unsettled us. There existed, of course, the gruesome stories about severed heads stuck to Bumble Bee tuna cans and sawed-off frozen body parts. There was the futuristic vibe as well, the aura of stepping sideways into a science fiction plot, something out of *The X-Files* or *Alien*. We were entering a space where people focused intensely on the future—cryonicists often liken themselves to space travelers, hence the term *cryonauts*—but from a perspective rooted in the past, where the means and practices for reaching that future seemed medieval and macabre. Yet what frightened me the most, what seemed not just surreal but downright unnatural, was that I believed I was going to a place that ran counter to the human body's most natural instinct. I thought of my father and his seizures, his craniectomy, and how when a quarter of his skull was removed, his brain seemed to breathe of its own accord. I thought of how his body was sending a message, however much I didn't want it to, that it bore intolerable pain and wanted to rest. I thought how life meant death: that this was what we've been told everywhere, all the time, as long as we've been alive.

How then did a group of people convince itself so thoroughly of the opposite?

∞

Cryonicists argue that death is a relative term. The Cryonics Paradigm, a theory first formulated by Robert Ettinger, the so-called Father of Cryonics, proposes that our current definitions of death are inadequate and crucially dependent on available technologies. Alcor maintains dual claims: that life can stop and start as long as a basic biological structure is preserved and that, through its research and breakthroughs, Alcor has harnessed the technology for that preservation.

On a basic level, our definition of death does change. Life may carry on in unexpected ways. We no longer assume, for example, that when breathing and blood circulation stop, life stops as well. Suffer a heart attack and you may still survive more than ten minutes of cardiac arrest. Slip under a frozen stream in Sweden and hypothermia might slow you down so that you survive eighty minutes underwater.

Death can fool us. Cryonicists merely ask we delay its declaration until "information-theoretic death" occurs: that is, only when the brain's information and memory become irretrievable should one consider a human life lost.

Cryonics is an experiment, Alcor says. We go into life knowing only that it results in death, so why not go into death hoping that it might result in life?

To our left the Scottsdale airport stretched back, charter planes dotting the tarmac. A landscaping crew worked along its fence. Our blue dot hovered over Alcor's red pin on the GPS and we parked on the street. Paloverdes and red birds-of-paradise lined the road, alongside rows of shrubbery trimmed to look like poodles. It was hard to tell if we were in the city proper; everything in Scottsdale appeared also outside Scottsdale. The office buildings had unforthcoming names like PCA Skin and Kyocera. Alcor, with its futuristic ring, was named after a distant star in the Big Dipper, one so faint in the night sky it was said that only someone with excellent eyesight could spot it.

Alcor's gray, single-story building was largely windowless; on either side, two squat towers jutted out like rooks. The anonymity felt intentional, almost clandestine. A few cars were parked in its lot and the front door was locked with a note telling visitors to ring the doorbell. We hesitated. "This is weird," Bree said. She took a picture of the facade and uploaded it to Instagram. "Would it be wrong if I made the hashtag *Popsicles*?"

We entered an empty lobby. A couch and some chairs sat around a glass coffee table with *Cryonics*, a monthly newsletter, fanned across it. Grainy portraits of men and women lined the walls, a name and date of birth under each. A cubicle crowded the middle of the room, as if lugged in from another office and then forgotten. Someone had cut out newspaper cartoons of cryonics jokes and pasted them to the cubicle wall: "I'm beginning to think this whole cryonics thing was a mistake," one shivering angel said to another. The word *Alcor* appeared in large blue letters on the cubicle wall. The wife of a board member recently refurbished the lobby, but for now the décor suggested it had gone untouched since the '70s.

A woman stepped out of the office as we started to wonder if there was anyone there at all. She was very tall, her hair swung across her back in a braided ponytail, and she had one of the longest faces I'd ever seen. Her eyes drooped high up on her forehead; her nose ran the length of my index finger. Her face was strangely handsome, like something you might find on an old Roman coin. She spoke to us in a loud, soothing whisper, telling us her name was Diane and that, although she usually handled sales and membership, the CEO and head technician weren't there so she would lead us on our tour. We should have a seat and relax. Two more would be joining us and then we'd begin.

The problem with the Cryonics Paradigm is that it's one thing to delay death and another to return life. Alcor bases its premise for reviving bodies from cryostasis upon the belief that "methods of repairing structure at the molecular level" are now foreseen. Through nanotechnology, the building of matter on the atomic level, cryonicists anticipate our ability to grow and manipulate individual atoms to reform a human body from scratch. The reformation process, however, remains highly theoretical.

This conviction in scientific progress' inexorable march forms a core tenet of transhumanism, the underlying philosophy of cryonics. Transhumanism argues that human intelligence constitutes a separate and more powerful force than humanity itself and so, by the end of the twenty-first century, it's reasonable to think humans will no longer be the most capable or intelligent beings on the planet. The machines we've designed will hold that distinction instead.

Cryonics has had a long history rooted in science fiction.

When Robert Ettinger outlined the idea for it in his 1962 book *The Prospect of Immortality*, he did so after reading "The Jameson Satellite," a story published in 1931 in which the last man on earth preserves his body by orbiting in a space capsule for forty million years. But with the election of Max More, a prominent futurist advocate, as Alcor's CEO in 2011, these science fiction origins gave way to the artificial intelligence–based utopian visions of transhumanism. At this point, a movement that was once seen as the domain of DIY, tinkering-in-the-garage types attempted to gain mainstream traction.

Yet until it does, Alcor exists on the fringe. As long as it's positioned outside the dominant cultural and scientific institutions, cryonics will have trouble raising and maintaining money for both research and preservation.

This does not stop Alcor from presenting itself as affordable. It urges interested members to take out a life insurance policy so that cryonics becomes no more a living expense than, in Max More's words, a daily Starbucks latte. Still, a full-body cryopreservation costs a nonrefundable $200,000, and a neuro-cryopreservation costs $80,000 (*neuro* being the shorthand for a patient who wants only his head preserved—I say "his" because the percentage of male cryonauts overwhelms at 75 percent). On top of this, yearly membership dues add up to $550. Yet while that money goes to everything needed to cool and preserve the body as well as the establishment of a patient trust, it's impossible to estimate what the costs of waking and reintegrating the patient will be—a patient who, 200 years later, will possess an outdated skill and language set, not to mention most likely a need for therapy and psychological rehabilitation.

The most Alcor can do is promise it will be by your side, like some young boy-priest guarding a pharaoh's tomb. It promises that the members of its trust are not grave robbers or looters, but loved ones themselves, husbands and wives or sons and daughters of members in cryopreservation. You will enter a larger family as eager and invested to see the technology work as anyone else.

Which raises two questions. The first was Bree's. What happens if not the patients, but Alcor itself runs out of money?

And the second: What if the person who returns from cryostasis does not remember the person who first died? Are they, then, the same person?

A couple was buzzed in. They were blandly attractive, in their late twenties with well-kempt hair and clear, pink skin. They looked like they met at one of the nearby offices. They sat down on the couch. The man, I noticed, wore a thick silver wedding band. I was suspicious. Why were they here? What did they come for—to sign themselves up or to get a kick out of it?

I smiled and asked the man where they drove from. "Scottsdale," he said and then, as if the conversation needed further deadening, "Not far." I said it was hot out there. They agreed. I realized, rather self-consciously, that these two thought Bree and I were another couple interested in possibly exploring the joys of eternal life together. I covered my left hand with my right. Bree flipped through her magazine.

That this couple might have been prospective members opened up some questions. Namely, wasn't it selfish to cryonically freeze yourself? Didn't one have better uses for time and money and hopes? Maybe I was uncharitable, but wasn't there some mandate as a citizen of the world, one hopefully aware of its overpopulation and limited resources as well as its ongoing climate change and probable, if inevitable, vast environmental ruin, to accept the fact that you die and turn the world over to others? If Alcor was about seeing far and distantly into the future, about a grandness and boldness of vision that rivals the cosmonauts, then there was also a myopia here, an inability to see past one's self.

Most of all, I wanted to find out this: What runs through the mind of someone who wants to live forever? What sort of person would never want to die?

I wanted to know what happens when the cryo-men and -women wake up in the Arizona heat, travel the fifteen hours and four minutes it takes to drive from Scottsdale to the Kansas prairie, ride a creaking elevator 650 feet down into the earth, and then open their memory boxes in the vast and silent mine. I wanted to know what happens when the time vault unticks and the flood of memories appear and the smell of salt lingers in the mausoleum of what was once there. When loneliness creeps into that great, underground vastness and sidles up to them to whisper that although they're not dead, everything and everyone else they know is.

Diane led the four of us out a back door of the lobby, down a hallway, and into the operating room. A gurney sat in the room's middle. A mess of wires and tubing coiled around everything. The arrangement looked halfway between hospital room and lab.

Here newly dead cryonics patients underwent a process called perfusion. Alcor's doctors drained the body of its blood and water, butterflied open the patient's sternum, and attached cannulation tubes to the heart. They pumped in cryoprotectant solution, a cocktail of chemicals and water that spread throughout the circulatory system and maintained cellular structure. "It has thirty-seven ingredients and it took a long time to perfect. Not even we know everything that's in it," Diane said, making the solution sound a bit like Heinz 57.

Up until the last decade, Alcor perfused bodies with water instead of cryoprotectants, the difference being that cryoprotectants vitrify the body instead of freezing it. Frozen water forms ice crystals, which expand in the corpse and rupture the cell structure of internal organs. Vitrification preserves the body by cooling it down into a solid but unfrozen state. "It's like turning the body to glass," Diane told us. It becomes a cracked windshield yet to fracture, a latticework of fissures held in delicate stasis. The downside, as Max More explained, is that cryoprotectants equal a sort of medical-grade antifreeze, chemicals whose harm we don't yet know the full extent.

Farther back in the room, there was a smaller operating area with a large glass box sitting on a table. "That's for the neuros," Diane said.

Aaron Drake, Alcor's medical response director, often takes charge of the medical team for a neurocryopreservation. A paramedic firefighter from Lincoln, Nebraska, Drake is bald

and stocky yet muscular with that look of quick calm competence you wish for in emergency response. He begins a neuro
by shaving the patient's head and sterilizing the scalp. He cuts
two incisions on either side to expose the skull and peels the
skin back with forceps. He drills burr holes on either side—
small tunnels into the skull typically used to treat subdural hematomas—and then scrapes out bits of bone. A team member
inserts crackphones into these holes, instruments that measure
the perfusion process and warn if the brain's cells are in danger
of freezing. Once all this is ready, the head, as Diane euphemized, is "removed from the trunk." The medical team inserts
tubes carrying cryoprotectants into the patient's carotid arteries. If the head perfuses successfully, the brain retracts from
the skull an eighth of an inch. Alcor disposes the rest of the
body in one of three ways: cremation, burial, or deep-freezing,
according to the patient's wishes.

Neurocryopreservation appeals because there's less variability at stake: instead of having to monitor the transfusion
and levels of solution throughout the whole body and its various organs, only one organ needs attention, the one we believe
to be the seat of memory and consciousness. While a full body
perfusion lasts four days, a neuro only takes one; a lot more
can go wrong given the extra time. In addition, neuros are
cheaper and, if the patient is elderly, he is already banking on
nanotechnology's ability to grow a new body. On one of his
video tours, Max More, chipper and irritatingly fit in his black
blazer, points to his head and says, "I figure by the time I go, I
won't want to take this broken-down old body. Why not protect the important stuff, which is all up here?"

The process, however, remained in the works. "We just changed the way we do these," Diane informed us. "It used to be we severed at the fifth or sixth vertebra. Now it's at the ninth or tenth so there'll be a bit more trunk. The bosses thought there were some pretty important nerve endings down there they wanted to keep." When I asked what that meant for patients preserved the old way, Diane shrugged and said, "I don't know." Which was, of course, true. None of us did.

In Greek mythology, Zeus grants Tithonus, son of the king of Troy, eternal life upon his lover Aurora's request. But Aurora forgets to ask Zeus for eternal youth, and so Tithonus is doomed to age eternally. He withers so much he transforms into a cicada, rustling his wings in a plea for death.

From the operating room we walked to the conference room, passing photos of Alcor's preserved members along the walls. Individuals stood in more or less employee-of-the-month poses: heads and trunks, the limbo of a wan smile. Underneath each date of birth was not a date of death, but of cryopreservation.

One photo was of a cat. "Yes!" Diane brightened. "We preserve pets. That's the office cat. He liked to hang out upstairs. An Italian member just flew over to have his German shepherd frozen. Though, you know, we only do neuros for animals."

Another member photo had been photoshopped. The black-and-white face of a young man with a half-mullet haircut was wiped out, his features smoothed and fuzzed over. "What's up with that?" Bree asked.

"Oh, that guy. That's his driver license photo." Diane nodded. "The boss didn't think the original looked good, so he had it changed." Max More, it seemed, had already preempted nanotechnology.

In truth, I recognized the same tendency in myself. It grew easy to dehumanize anyone associated with cryonics. Diane, for instance, with her long face and unblinking eyes, struck me as singularly reptilian. She stood in the hallway, waiting for our questions in silence, tongue ready to dart out and catch a fly. In his airbrushed videos, Max More appeared just a tad too self-composed, as if you were watching a slightly malfunctioning robot that smiled too quickly at the thought of its own disembodied head. And the Scottsdale couple I'd already written off as Stepfords, ready for the moment when they shed their skin and extended long green tentacles toward Bree and myself.

In wishing a gift for Tithonus, Aurora accidentally damns the one she loved most. But perhaps more tellingly, in her fervency that her lover remain human, Aurora turns him into something else.

The conference room waited at the end of the hall. A long table stretched in the middle, desk chairs around it. Tinted windows looked out on the parking lot. To our right, a metal shutter was cut into the wall. This looked into the patient bay area. "Step on over," Diane beckoned. "Let's have a peek." She flipped a lever and the shutter cranked up.

We peered through the window on to a row of shining aluminum tanks extending from floor to ceiling, wide enough that all five of us would need to link arms to encircle one. They looked like the tanks you'd find on a tour of a brewery and, although they were behind glass, it was hard not to think about how much more accessible, how less guarded, these were than Alcor members' underground boxes of stuff. These were the dewars, and inside were the bodies.

Cryonauts are preserved at a temperature of -196 degrees Celsius. Diane pointed to the hoses attached to the tops of each container—these pumped a steady supply of liquid nitrogen to ensure the bodies stayed cool. Alcor keeps four bodies in a dewar at a time, each stored vertically in its own quadrant of space. The staff took the newly preserved body outside and then lowered it headfirst by crane from the roof into its open dewar.

"Head first?" The woman from Scottsdale curdled her lip, speaking for the first time. I was unsure why this detail offended her. "It's a preventative measure," Diane explained. "We don't anticipate it, but if we run out of liquid nitrogen, levels would decrease from the top down. So the first part of the body to be exposed would be the feet, instead of the head. And you don't want to lose your noggin."

"If there's a natural disaster," Diane assured us, "These dewars can run six to eight months on their own. They use almost no electricity, and the glass window that looks on to them is bulletproof." Alcor had hitched up a state-of-the-art alarm system throughout. "There are a lot of people out there who don't like cryonics or what we do," Diane explained, and nodded to the shatterproof window. "We have enough defenses here to withstand a full-fledged assault long enough for the police to arrive. We can't repel it, but we can survive it." She shook her head. "People want us to fail. One patient, his wife never even called to tell us he had died. She waited until it was too late. Think of that—his whole life's work, gone." Whether or not any imminent threat loomed, there's a rationale to the building's bunker-type mentality. It isn't just the body, but the structure and its containers that need preservation. Alcor relocated to Scottsdale from its original location outside San Francisco because it was looking for somewhere less likely to be hit by earthquakes and other environmental disasters over a long period of time.

Diane motioned us over to the conference table. A miniature dewar stood on it. It was a 3D printout, the handiwork of an employee who builds 3D printers on the side. "Go ahead and check it out," she smiled. Bree opened it. Inside were the different containers for the bodies and, in the center, sat what looked like a Pez dispenser. "What's this?" Bree asked, pulling it out. "Oh, that," Diane said offhandedly. "That's where we keep the neuros." Alcor keeps up to six heads in one dewar. Each is zipped up in a bag, then placed inside a tin bucket and stuck in its allotted slot on the vertical bar. Diane blinked. "Think of it like a totem pole."

Later, on the car ride back, Bree told me this was the moment for her. We both felt not quite right. Though we had talked beforehand about how we had strong stomachs, there we were and it was still weird. "I felt my body then," she said of that moment. "I'd never been so conscious of its weight."

The totem pole of heads made sense: it was economical, efficient, saved liquid nitrogen, and lowered upkeep. It made sense as well that the brains of cats and dogs were kept in the same dewars as people. "We don't have much room, so we put them wherever there's an open nook," said Max More. If you think about it, this wasn't all that different from burial and graveyard, columbarium or morgue. But still there was something off. My mind could process and rationalize the storage system, yet it felt, for lack of a better word, inhumane.

Why was that? What made me shudder? Bree was onto something. Imagine your head removed from "your trunk"— in what Alcor calls "a cephalic isolation procedure"—or the bone scraped clean from the burr holes. Imagine the coffee-ground emesis and hemorrhaging, the cool blue antifreeze washed through your body until it ate through the lining of your lungs. Or imagine watching someone you love go through this. It wasn't exactly the viscera that unnerved me, or the body's desecration; minus the decapitation, this trauma didn't differ all that much from what happens when, say, a car-accident victim is brought into the ER. Instead it was the sense of hope that threw me off, the violence that accompanied such wishful thinking. To see hope take this physical manifestation was to witness the force of that sentiment in all its gruesomeness.

Diane told us that the mother of an Australian man sends her preserved son letters every year for his birthday and Christmas. Alcor keeps them so that he may read them when he wakes up. The mother is not a member and so knows they'll never meet again but, hopefully, some sort of natural order will be restored: in some sense, the son will be able to outlive his mother.

The night before my father died, I turned out the lights and walked out of his hospital room and made the mistake of looking back before I closed the door. I saw his body propped up on the bed, his shrunken torso and caved-in head, and I realized he would have to go through the night alone. It seemed wrong he would die: I had just turned twenty, he had just turned fifty-nine, and this was not, I was convinced, how life turned into death. But the despondency of leaving him alone rubbed up against the instinct for movement, to walk out the door and translate this moment into memory to be stored in some deeply hidden and secure box. In these dewars, with their silent, waiting bodies, I recognized that same despondency without any movement. There was no room in them for grief or mourning. To delay the acceptance of what's lost harms the lives that survive that loss. *Death* remains one of the few words I can think of for which the adjective *universal* actually holds. How lonely would it be to want to exist outside of that?

"We have some really unique members," Diane said back in the conference room, referring to the bodies on the other side of the glass. She laid out brochures and an introductory handout as part of her soft pitch. Bree and I shared one, as did the Scottsdales across the table. Diane asked us to consider joining. "A Catholic nun. A 101-year-old. Some Chinese. A lot of Quebecois. A Holocaust survivor with the numbers, you know . . ." Diane searched for the word. "Tattooed," said the man from Scottsdale. "Yes, the numbers tattooed on her arm," she continued. "You know, people in the future will want to talk with her and see about all the barbaric behavior that went on in the past."

"Some others would be less useful to talk to. Less educational," Diane confided. "We have some problems with mental health here. Some people who don't get out very much. Sometimes people call the office just for conversation and it's my job to talk to them. They're not even members; they just want someone to talk to. One man from Spain does that a lot," she trailed off. "But we're full of really interesting people. We even have a few transgender cases. Although they're only neuros. Too bad because it would have been so interesting for people from the future to study them."

Disregarding the insensitivity of her lab-experiment approach, Diane raised an interesting consideration: That the mind of a person who came back might not necessarily want the same body beneath it. One's new identity might in fact be tethered to the idea of changing one's old one. Could cryonics refashion or reinterpret our identity to find a more aligned version of ourselves? And would that new version be someone more or less ourselves?

I couldn't help but think of Patient #124, whose log I read on Alcor's website. On a Tuesday morning in May 2014, Patient #124 called Alcor's Scottsdale office from Alabama, saying he had been shot by an intruder. It was soon clear this wasn't true; Patient #124 had not been shot but was intending to shoot himself. He had taken a large dose of sleeping pills and called his family members. Now he was informing Alcor to come get him. But when Patient #124 heard police sirens, he hung up and shot himself in the chest. Alcor filed an injunction to block the autopsy, and team members flew out, did a field washout, performed a neuro separation, and flew the head back by two in the morning. What desperation drove #124 to do this? More than that, what desperation would make him want to return?

Here, memory boxes played their part. Each Alcor member had access to a box they could fill, update, and store in the Kansas subterrain. The boxes were their fail-safes, a patient's constant. A memory box supposed that what composes a life connects inextricably to the contents of that life. We are who we are because of what we had. And so when a box was opened, its contents would release a flood of memories—an electroshock of nostalgia—and the shorthand of a past life would appear.

One man filled his memory box with his own composed music, figuring it would finally be appreciated by the time he returned. Another requested a digital memory box, betting this would outlast the half-life of paper and Polaroids (although one's tempted to ask if a CD-ROM drive or USB port will be at all accessible 200 years from now). Another woman encrypted DVDs made of stone with old Christmas photos and letters. A software engineer planned to bring along his grandfather's silver bolo tie, a collection of Kurosawa films, and a copy of *Doom*. "We don't know how memory will work," Diane said. "But we think these might bring people back to who they are."

∞

There's a Voltaire quote, favored by cryonicists, that goes: "To rise again—to be the same person that you were—you must have your memory perfectly fresh and present; for it is memory that makes your identity. If your memory be lost, how will you be the same man?" The problem is, in order to determine if a person's memory will be fresh, present, or lost, we first have to be certain about how memory works. As Diane pointed out, memory is notoriously mysterious and difficult to pinpoint. "The brain is an interconnective mechanism and so memory's a distributed thing," said Bruce Hansen, a ponytailed neuroscientist I talked to at Colgate University. "In order to replay it, you have to run it through the areas that did the initial processing."

But what if, as Max More put it, "the important stuff" is not all "up there" in the head? The stomach's been found to contain over 100,000 neurons as well as 95 percent of the body's serotonin, a neurotransmitter. The heart holds over 40,000 neurons and inhibits or facilitates electrical activity in the brain. While Alcor researchers recently made a breakthrough in determining that long-term memories remained intact in nematode worms after freezing, we still have no idea how a human brain would respond to such a change much less the rest of the body.

Memory boxes might have one thing to their advantage. "There's a theory, attractive but still unproven," Hansen said, "that our ability to perceive surroundings is based on our memories. Our context, our experiences, our moods lead us to have unconscious expectations. And the new features we perceive happen because we're tapping into stores of memories."

If context then shapes our perceptions, could that work in the reverse? If we were a freshly revived cryonaut, could seeing a familiar face in a photo help retrieve our memory?

"Well sure, you could say that," Hansen continued. "Just don't get carried away."

As for a life worthy or unworthy of living, Diane couldn't see why anyone would want to return and then not keep living. She asked us to imagine it—you could come back and choose to live at any age you please with your loved ones, free of disease or death. "Most Alcor members choose their twenties," she added with a wink toward me and Scottsdale guy. Nanotechnology, she said, would be just like Botox: a tightening up. Anything would be possible. Who would say no to more of life? I asked about Patient #124. "Well, things can always change," Diane responded. "He might feel differently when he comes back. Just remember, don't shoot yourself in the head."

From the Alcor conference room, we headed to a second operating room, filing through an underlit hallway with more photos along the wall.

Here there hung a photo of Fred Chamberlain Jr., the father of Fred Chamberlain III who founded Alcor in the early 1970s along with his wife, Linda. Fred Jr. was Alcor's first neurocryopreservation case in 1976, when the company consisted of only five members. Fred III performed the surgery in a two-bedroom California apartment turned impromptu operating room, the procedure hurried along by Fred Jr.'s declining condition.

As far as origin stories, Alcor's was initially a race against time, a journey as far as possible to bring a father back and save a sick and damaged head. That the neuro procedures and preservation methods were still rudimentary, that the head was most likely separated at the wrong vertebra, and that there is now, realistically, no chance of Fred Jr. ever returning, fell beside the point. Diane grimaced and admitted as much when I asked her.

But still the possibility of Fred Jr.'s return tantalized me. It would be like giving birth—Fred III cooling his father's head out of cryostasis—something out of Greek myth but rewritten, a future from the past.

When I was younger and believed in a heaven hidden in great white clouds, I daydreamed it as a great reunion: as long as I didn't do anything too bad, I would show up and there I'd run across all the loved ones I had lost in life. The logistics at first troubled me—what if I were old and my father and grandparents, who had only known me when I was young, didn't recognize me? What if they were still as sick as when they died or we had become strangers in the intervening years? What would I hold in my memory box to help remember them? But then suddenly these concerns no longer mattered. This was heaven, after all: the future would work the past out for itself.

∞

This idea of heaven and Alcor doesn't seem so far off. At a certain point, cryonics turns from science to religion. Several members indeed list it as such on their profiles. The decision to sign up seems not so much a faith in humanity as it is in a higher power: the transhumanist notion that human intelligence can create a sort of divinity. There's logic and science behind cryonics, but there's also a point where logic reduces enough so that probability, in cryonicists' own estimates, fades into the unknown. And that's closer to faith.

After my tour, I talked to Jay Lewis, a software engineer living in Phoenix. In 2006, while in his mid-thirties, doctors misdiagnosed Jay with an enlarged heart. He spent several days in a hospital bed, undergoing tests and reflecting on his life. His condition turned out to be caused by a chlorine allergy but still he started researching anti-aging methods. Eventually he landed on Alcor. He attended a conference in nearby Scottsdale and, to his surprise, the people he encountered gave smart, logical arguments. When I spoke with Jay over the phone, he told me: "You'd think there'd be more, but only a couple people there seemed crazy. It got me interested. It seemed plausible. I mean bacteria are practically immortal." A few years later, he took out an insurance policy and signed up as a full-body member with Alcor. His fiancée was also a member; they met at a conference, her stipulation being that she only date other cryonicists. The previous year they froze their dog Nutmeg, a fourteen-year-old Australian shepherd, and Jay hoped he'd live long enough to see her unfrozen.

When I asked Jay what he looked forward to with cryonics, I did not anticipate his answer. "I'm excited to travel to other solar systems," he said. "If you think about it, once the technology expands, we'll be able to put people in and out of cryonics at will." It was historic, a word Jay liked to use, in two senses: you'd not only be one of the first humans to prolong life through cryonics but you'd be able to witness events as an ancestor to them. Jay went on: "Imagine when we colonize the next solar system. That could take one hundred, even one thousand years to reach. With cryonics, we could freeze people for that and they would awaken when they reached their destination. We'd become time travelers. The technical possibilities excite me, the ones that don't have anything to do with avoiding death. Say you wake up in the future and you're bored. You could save up a lot of money, invest it, and then sign up for a hundred-year sleep. You wake up and you'll be richer. You could see how all your favorite cities have changed."

I told Jay it sounded like immortality with a fast-forward button, but I didn't say what I really thought: that this seemed, if not delusional, then a strange mixture of conviction and hope. That, like Patient #124, the future was being used as a way to assuage or excuse the present.

I asked instead if Jay thought this might not work out. He stopped himself: "Well, what if no one wants to wake me up? What's my skill set? I'm just a software engineer. That might not warrant my getting the best resuscitation method. And you'd want to go with some people but who decides who goes? If you take 500 of your friends, then each of them would want to take another couple hundred. But if you went alone, then it'd be a form of suicide. Your friends would have to wait a long while."

None of his friends or family were upset with his choice, but Jay encountered resistance when he tried to recruit others to do it. "It seems like it wouldn't be that hard," he told me. "People convert religions all the time. Pagans to Christians, Christians to Scientologists. But cryonics is more functionally like an insurance policy. You don't need to abandon a set of beliefs. Why wouldn't you do it? You're offering someone a 10 percent chance they wouldn't die, something that would happen anyway." Jay paused. Then he asked, "Have you talked with anyone that's been able to sign people up? Do you know what they said?"

I told him, honestly, I hadn't.

In Alcor's second operating room, we crowded around another gurney with a mannequin on it. A 3D printer stood against the wall. Its progeny, a printout of a very large owl, sat on a shelf overlooking the room. It was missing, perhaps fittingly, the top half of its head.

The mannequin lay inside an open body bag, blue plastic cubes around him. "That's the ice we use to cool the patient down in the field," Diane said. "It's like the inside of a bean-bag chair." The dummy comes hooked up to all the machinery needed for a field washout, a black rubber cooling mask stretched over the upper half of its face. Diane called this the Batman mask. She let me take a picture of it.

A patient's last hours often become a race. If Alcor doesn't reach a patient within twenty-four hours of death, edema and irreversible swelling set in. And while Alcor's bullish about the endurance of chemical information in brain tissue (neurons are sometimes cultured as long as four to eight hours after death), it's nevertheless imperative to begin cooling the brain at once. If after permanent cardiac arrest Alcor does not restore blood circulation and breathing within fifteen minutes, the patient is irretrievable as well.

How, when, and where we die is important. In its ideal world, Alcor would treat its patients in-house, easing them into and controlling their time of death. As it stands, Alcor must negotiate the uncertain health and critical state of its members to ensure that Aaron Drake and his team reach the body in time. If the patient doesn't die in Scottsdale, Alcor navigates the terrain of unfamiliar hospitals and potentially unsympathetic doctors. They file injunctions against autopsies, contact local funeral directors, catch last-minute flights, carve out a space in the hospital to work, and plead with hospital staff to keep patients on life support.

But for all its seemingly idyllic security, Scottsdale provides one great problem: the heat. If a patient dies out of state, he's usually flown in through commercial airliner. Though the Scottsdale airport is tantalizingly close, these flights are mandated to arrive into Phoenix's Sky Harbor Airport. Because Alcor is a nonprofit and not a licensed mortuary, it's not allowed to transport dead bodies back to its headquarters on its own. So Alcor has licensed a nearby funeral home to do so on their behalf. Phoenix, however, posts such high temperatures during the summer that law requires that remains travel only at night. During the day, the body carries too great a chance of decomposing. So the corpse, cooled down with its Batman mask and its body bag full of dry ice, must sit around till night before it can be transported back. And as Bree and I knew, it gets sweaty.

We returned to the lobby. The tour was almost over. Diane gathered us around a glass chamber built into the wall. Inside a horizontal cylinder stretched back, deep enough to hold a body, something like an MRI scanner. The cylinder was dark, though lights twinkled inside it, stars perhaps, miniature Alcors like the lights that line theater aisles so you can see your way through the dark.

We stared into the tunnel, all five of us. "You're looking into the future," Diane said. It was a rehearsed line, the kind you could tell she used to wrap up a tour. True, the lights did look a bit like stars, like some great and beckoning adventure, but mostly we saw our own reflections. I pointed that out and Scottsdale guy beamed with the irony.

If cryonics is a matter of faith, then like other religions, there is a group getting saved and a group left out. Alcor claims everyone can sign up—it even posts articles online theorizing how "Really Big Dewars" capable of holding millions of heads will be feasible and cheap to build one day—but that *everyone* is a slippery, hardly inclusive term. At the same time that cryonics and transhumanism make wonderfully expansive points about the human capacity for intelligence and achievement, they also make, whether they want to or not, certain choices about which humans should benefit from those capacities. The price tag remains $80,000 for a head and $200,000 for the whole body. Again, this is not necessarily its members' fault; if cryonics were more mainstream, the expense might prove less an issue. But I couldn't help but think of the advanced alarm system, the shatterproof glass, the bulletproof window, and the way the Scottsdale guy nodded when Diane mentioned federal bureaucracy and Alcor's team of wealthy Florida investors dedicated to finding nonprofit tax loopholes.

I thought of this too even within Alcor. Jay Lewis worried that he wouldn't have the historic value or support system there to wake him up. "Maybe they'll need a guy who's able to show people how things were done a hundred or a thousand years ago. A historical reenactor. That could be me," he said. "The culture will have changed so much it'll be like coming to another country—maybe some other cryos will wake me up since, you know, expats tend to stick with other expats."

Perhaps the question wasn't whether you'll live forever, but whether you've been deemed worthy of it. There's a rich and a meek on the other side of Alcor's windows, VIPs and historical reenactors, though it seemed, if cryonics worked, that only one would be around to inherit the earth.

The Scottsdale couple shook Diane's hand and left, but Bree and I stuck around. I rifled through the cryonics magazines. Bree asked Diane how she started working there. "Well, I used to work in healthcare, administrative stuff. Then I had five kids and I couldn't anymore. But my husband had a heart attack when he was forty-eight. I had to go back to work and so I started here."

"What does your husband think about your job?" Bree asked.

"Oh, he thinks it's nuts. He doesn't believe in the whole cryonics thing."

I put the magazine back on the rack and looked at the photo of a woman on the wall outside Diane's office. This was one of the yet-to-be-preserved patients, the wife of a board member. Diane walked over and stood next to it.

"She looks just like my mother. I asked for it to be placed there so I could see her whenever I walked in. She had hair just like that." Diane swung her own braid around to gaze at the picture.

I wondered if Diane was one of the seven employees to be signed up, whether she thought some part of her would take this woman for her mother should they both come back. And perhaps this woman would treat Diane as her own daughter. Maybe this was the face that would go into Diane's memory box and return her to herself. But at the same time, why didn't she just keep a photo of her actual mother in her actual office?

A week after our tour, I met Richard Leis in a coffee shop near campus. One of Bree's students from her undergraduate poetry workshop, Richard had raised his hand when Bree told her class about our visit and showed her his membership bracelet.

Richard was wearing his bracelet as I stood up to shake his hand. He worked at the University of Arizona as a specialist for the Mars Global Surveyor Orbiter Camera and, in his late thirties, he was finishing up his undergraduate degree. He was balding and his graying hair was kept short, but there seemed something endearingly childlike about him. He ordered a hot chocolate on a hot day. He still wore braces ("Though he's about to get them off!" Bree insisted). Richard said he wrote mostly unrequited love poems and then laughed. He'd won the undergraduate award for poetry, and later, Bree quoted me one poem's opening: "I am not the type of man who can wear a hat."

Richard said he'd contemplated the idea of cryonics since childhood. He fell in love with pseudoscience—Bigfoot, UFOs, time machines—and when he was unhappy in college, he survived by listening to *Coast to Coast*, a radio show that specialized in fringe theories. It was the same path by which many cryonauts came to Alcor: an interest that originated in a cultural fascination with science fiction.

When I asked Richard what he planned to do when he was unfrozen, he said realistically he didn't expect he would be. "I had enough money to do one weird thing with my life and this was it. It's just a temporary storage space. In a sense, I don't care where you put me. I just thought there should be another option besides burial and cremation."

But while Diane trumpeted Alcor's lowered dues, the company also required its longer-termed members such as Richard—who signed up back when full-body preservations only cost $150,000—to pay the $50,000 difference when the cost rose to $200,000. Some members pulled out, sacrificing what they had already spent; Richard stayed in and increased his life insurance.

As for a memory box, Richard didn't want one. "When I

was younger, I moved around the country a lot. I had to practice cutting off friendships, starting new in an unfamiliar place. I lived in Rochester, Oregon, Salt Lake, Phoenix, Tucson. I've grown to appreciate that disconnect. I'm not a collector; I'm not inclined to collect. I want whatever this pattern is here to continue on," he moved his hands over his chest. "I want this consciousness to come back with me. If another me came back, then I wouldn't have avoided death at all."

It was back to that original, romantic notion of cryonics: of life and death as a grand experiment, and human life an experiment in form. Richard talked about taking beginner's Spanish at the U of A. His professor was explaining the difference between *ser* and *estar*—the two different words for "to be"—one that applies to a temporary state or action, *estar*, and one that implies a more permanent one, *ser*. He'd used *ser* for everything, ascribing all actions permanence, and realized that he needed to start using *estar*. This, to him, was what cryonics and suspended animation were capable of doing: they make us reevaluate what we previously considered final.

When Bree and I drove back to Tucson, we kept to ourselves. Bree marked up poems for class and we discussed her thesis, a book of poems about the different heirlooms hidden throughout her family home in Pennsylvania, a house built in the 1700s.

We talked about what we'd put in our memory boxes. Bree said she kept imagining them and all she could picture was takeout menus and concert tickets.

"It makes me think about what I keep," she said. "I have a

collection of movie tickets. Of every single movie I've been to since 2005. Lela thinks it's silly. And I can see how she's right."

Jay Lewis, the owner of the Kurosawa films, the first edition of *Doom*, the nanotechnology magazines, and the bolo tie made by his silversmith grandfather, plans to have two memory boxes. He will digitize three black-and-white photo albums belonging to his grandmother, pictures taken from an era near the camera's invention. Then he'll include the souvenirs from a two-week solo backpacking trip he took to Europe in his early twenties, the booklets and guides from museums in Austria, Germany, and Switzerland, that he sometimes leafs through to remember what he saw.

I thought of all the people who signed up for Alcor. Patient #124. The holocaust survivor. The eighty-one-year-old man who paid an extra $50,000 to sign his wife and mother up against their wishes after they had died. Kim Suozzi, who died of an inoperable brain tumor at the age of twenty-three. The new mother who signed her and her child up after a difficult childbirth. The spouses who say don't wake me up without the other. The spouses who say do. Robert Ettinger, who froze both his first and second wife. The mother who sends her preserved son birthday cards.

The future Alcor promised was one that saved the past. It used cryonics as a way to rectify the ways we think life should have gone. Founder Fred Chamberlain severs his father's head in order to preserve his life. Jay Lewis finds himself awake and realizes someone has cared enough to be there on the other side to bring him back to life and that now, clambering aboard the spaceship to take him and his friends to the outer solar systems and their unending starlight, he has become both pioneer of the future and curator of the past. Maybe the tenet behind cryonics isn't that life is so grand one would never want to give it up. Maybe, just maybe, it's that life hasn't been grand enough.

I still dream of my father, years after his death, and when I do, I am always surprised to see him. He looks better—he walks, even talks, and I may put my arms around him. His brain is healed, his memory restored, the tumor miraculously shrunk and washed away. His skull bears no signs of the surgeries it endured: no scars, no burr holes, no sense of something incredibly hard cracked and given way to something incredibly soft. His hair has grown back. His speech has returned too, still slurred from paralysis, and in my dream I hear the gentle unexpected Brazilian accent.

I see him and I ask, "Where did you come from?" And sometimes he tells me he's back and he's better. Other times he tells me he was always here, that he never left. Afterward we struggle for things to say. We sit in our quiet home and wonder if we should heat up some bouillon and rice for dinner or turn on the TV. It's my conception of heaven projected five minutes further. Something is not right; in the intervening years, we've forgotten who we are. There's joy in the dream, the feeling that one could not ask for more from the world, but something else haunts it, an uncertainty or hesitation. He is and is not my father. I am and am not his son.

In the dream, I see signs of his illness's past—momentarily, he will fall silent and I will think the seizure's happening all over again, that now he will look into my eyes and crumple to the ground. I want to warn him that it will happen again. I want to warn him that my wish was a mistake, that I never should have hoped for this. I want to warn him to go away; I want to warn myself that too. He must leave again before the sickness appears and, this time, he must never return. Because if he kept coming back again, over and over, it would not be heaven but hell. Yet I also know that there's not much point in my saying this. This dream and his return will come back for as long as I live, as long as I should live, which will hopefully be not a minute longer than my memory binds me to a body and a mind.

CODA, CODEX

On our better days, we and the tree seem alike. Apollo chases Daphne and Daphne turns to laurel. Hades abducts Leuce and there she pops up again, a *Populus alba* in the Elysian Fields. Zeus gives his temple tenders, Baucis and Philemon, the gift of dying concurrently, and they shake green leaves and mossy lips until husband and wife become a linden and oak that stand so close together their branches twist from a single trunk.

This is not just tree transformation—Dante's suicides reliving an eternal shrubbery—but tree storage. In Arthurian legend, the Lady of the Lake entombs poor, besotted Merlin in a tree trunk. In Scandinavia, the oak's said to belong to the dead, not just because it was material for coffins, but because it was a coffin itself. Norsemen would search the woods until they crossed a suitable find, and there they'd bury their loved ones in the slingshot split of its trunk.

The Norse also said the gods whittled Eubla, the first woman, from oak. Virgil claimed oaks gave birth to the first men. When my mother likes to reference the Welsh in her, she will say, "I'm of druid stock." She's joking about that moony streak, the Merlin in her, but what she's really saying (the word *druid* stemming from *daur*, the Celtic for *oak*) is that she's made of wood.

So, a proposal: if you're looking for ways to stick around, there are worse fates than coming back as a tree.

A few summers ago, I worked as a wood splitter for a man named Angelo Romeo. This was Tucson, one hundred degrees, and I'd show up to Angelo's backyard at six thirty or so and work till noon. When the heat became too much to bear, I biked my way back over the pavement built by the WPA until I reached the closest air-conditioned space with energy drinks and a Panda Express.

My job was simple: to break down the rounds of wood Angelo collected from his tree service details around Tucson and stack them against a corrugated shed. We were essentially recycling, turning what was going to the dump into ethically sourced, locally harvested firewood to be bundled and sold at marked-up prices to Whole Foods. I used a machine splitter and built a wall of wood: mesquite, pine, pepper, china berry, birch.

Angelo's backyard was a cluttered place—a wood chipper hitched to a truck, a flatbed for hauling rounds, two splitters, a tarped-over workstation. Arborists' tools hung homicidally from the shed's walls: pole saws, chain saws, loppers, alarmingly large pruning shears. Red Baron pizza and flank steak in the freezer, OSHA regulations stapled to the wall. And throughout the yard, there were piles and piles of wood, wood strewn everywhere, wood that I, Sisyphus, would eventually split into smaller and smaller pieces. In one corner, Angelo even kept a pile for the "funny" shapes: the knots and gnarls and human faces in the warp of the trunk, the totem carved out of a round of mesquite, its face placid and content as it watched over me and my wall, protecting us from harm.

When he didn't work trees, Angelo was a firefighter. His looks matched his soap opera name: tan, dark hair, eyes like lakes. Two indentations sat on either temple, like dimples, as if a very small and very round hammer had pocked them there.

As far as bosses go, Angelo was a good one. He set up a fan to blow the exhaust away from where I worked. He climbed a ladder and stretched a blue tarp out back of the shed where I'd take unscheduled breaks to eat Lärabars in the shade. When I threw out my back because I lifted rounds the wrong way, he left me a brace and a blanket on which to rest my knees. He shooed away the tabby that liked to sidle up and scratch. When he saw me sweeping up palm fronds, he said, quite kindly, "Well, you see, Thomas, the trick is not to sweep like a pussy." I made ten dollars an hour and the mini-fridge, plastered with custom magnets reading *Romeo Tree Service, Baby!*, was always well-stocked with Powerade.

To help pass the time, I thought of my wall of wood as like

the wall of the Grand Canyon: the different varieties of trees formed a vast and magnificent patchwork, all layered on top of one another like the strata of rocks inside the canyon rim, the pre-Anthropocene layers you'd gaze at after slotting a quarter into parking-meter binoculars. Paleozoic, Precambrian, Vishnu. The Great Unconformity. The downside was that I became so carried away with seeing my wall as something else that I failed to create a stable structure. It sagged and split apart, under siege from its own weight. I quickly learned the structural limitations of a trapezoid as opposed to a rectangle. I had stacked so high and so dangerously that Angelo forbade his wife and daughter from walking underneath. He made me lug the splitter back another foot so that if the wall fell, it would not fall on me. Even the cat didn't saunter back there.

My job, if you were being generous, was a kind of architecture. Here I was, to break up the discarded and find a new and useful arrangement.

Whenever a tree trunk is chainsawed down, certain features surface. Rub a thumb over each ring and you can spot the rainy year, the dry year, the year of rot or fire or flood. The ever-higher carbon ratios, the contaminants in the water, the year a mesquite owner finally noticed the termite infestation and called a firefighter to perform cosmetics. The year a god tried to pluck all a girl's leaves. Wood absorbs a portion of everything we exhale (lungs, chimney smoke, a car's exhaust) and so stores it away in that year's ring. Cut it open and you butterfly its history. As far as memory goes, trees possess one to be trusted. If we ever want an objective record of the way things might have been, all we have to do is palm open our switchblades and find a leafy neighbor.

As it turned out, my wall never did fall. The most dangerous part of my job was the wood splitter: a machine made up of a small diesel engine, a cylindrical piston to latch onto the wood, and a sharp wedged blade. The closest comparison I can come up with is a medieval torture device with the horsepower of a lawnmower.

The job came without health insurance and so Angelo would lecture me very carefully on the importance of positioning my hands with regards to the splitter. I was to keep them on top of the log at all times and never on its sides. If I put my hands directly in line with the splitter's blade or cylinder, an errant glove-thread might snag or my hand might slip and mangle. A tree never fully heals and so its rings never fully forget—they grow around their wounds and scars, incorporating them into their past as imperfections and blemishes. One never knows when one of these would catch and cause a hand to fall in line with the blade. One must be respectful, Angelo motioned toward the log, of the things that were more powerful than us.

When Angelo took to the splitter, he moved quickly. He'd bend down toward a log twice the thickness of his thigh, embrace it, then heave against it for momentum. Once the log rolled onto the bar, he held its weight against his leg and yanked the lever. He split the wood down the middle and let one half fall to the ground. In short, expert strokes, he pushed the other half back and yanked the lever again, rotating the trunk to shave off individual pieces of firewood.

When the blade split the stump in two, the wood would make any number of sounds. Each log had its own personality, depending on its density, dryness, and age. Eucalyptus crumbled. Mesquite quartered into symmetrical chunks. Dry pine popped; wet pine pasted. Some pieces split silently and some cracked like a pistol shot. Some hissed or wheezed or shattered. Sometimes I'd find termite larvae burrowed into the pockets of wood, columbaria stacked throughout the striations and rings, and I'd gather the squishy little things in my glove and toss them over my shoulder like rice at a wedding, to clear the wall and land a treat for the starlings in the alleyway behind me.

Then there were the rule breakers, the anomalies. The logs that, for whatever reason—a hidden knot, an unseen tumorous growth—snapped back at my face, as if acting out some old grudge between us. At times, stripping a round off the blade was like flaying open veins and arteries, the edges of a quartered mesquite just like the marbled fat of flesh.

Other times, a log would groan something ancient and primordial, battered and hurt. I don't know much about the last sounds people make before they die, but I can tell you the sound of that wood being split was a distinctly human sound. I would look at the log after—the fan whirring, the starlings chirping on their wire—and it seemed I was making a sacrifice. It was the sound you'd make if you weren't fully aware of being human, if you had turned over in your sleep and, in your half-state, groaned about your very bad back. For a brief instant, Angelo yanking the lever, me hugging the next round for dear life, the wall growing ever higher, the sound wasn't the wood being split but the years themselves.

Occasionally, my girlfriend and I will argue about feng shui. I have no eye for it, it seems. Lamps in the corners. Sun on the desk. Don't sit with your back to the door. At least one leg of each chair should touch the rug. Clear pathways to all exits.

I say things should go anywhere. I stack my library willy-nilly in the built-in bookshelves. Pile my coffee table books not just on the coffee table. Together we've laid siege to the mantelpiece: a page from an illuminated manuscript, a black-and-white photo of swaying palm trees, a daguerreotype of her great-great-grandparents, a postcard of Titian, a book on New York City's trees, a photo of her and her sister, a mounted butterfly, my grandmother and her crossed legs, a cactus, a shell, a very large pinecone, some bones, a montage: my father, my father holding the dog, my father and me fishing in the Adirondacks, my father and me rowing a boat, my father and mother, whittled from oak, standing on a dock at sunset, my father alive.

Of course, feng shui encompasses more than just potpourri and hanging plants. It's the science of siting, a system of laws used to orient and arrange space, a practice that includes the search for the correct location for a tomb. This is, the pun goes, a grave matter: an auspicious or inauspiciously placed tomb could affect the deceased's family's fortunes for generations. When it comes down to it, what we argue about is the safest way to preserve the dead.

For instance, if you're burying a body in a cemetery, what is the best way to let a corpse decompose? If left to their own devices, bacteria will digest our cells at the meeting of the small and large intestines. A greenish patch will blister on our belly, and putrefaction will spread across our stomach, up our chest, and down our thighs. Autolysis occurs, first in the liver and brain, and enzymes break down our cells. Soft tissues melt into gases and liquids. Our body might push our intestines out our rectum. Our skin blackens. We bloat and ferment.

But how fast we do decompose depends on conditions. A body left exposed decays twice as fast as a body in water, eight times as fast as a body underground. Maggots can consume an exposed body so ferociously that their migration paths to and from the corpse leave divots in the soil. A body buried underground will take longer to decompose depending on whether it's embalmed or on what type of wood is used to make the coffin; an oak coffin, for example, is said to keep a corpse intact for fifty years. Inevitably, though, liquefied tissue will move from body to soil, and leach mercury, nitrogen, and other nutrients into its immediate surroundings. Lead and zinc from the casket lining will poach the earth as well; so too does the arsenic in the coffin wood's preservatives, the formaldehyde in embalming fluids. We become part of what a 2015 *Guardian* article on the science of decomposition terms "the cadaveric ecosystem," releasing, on average, the 64 percent of us that's water, the 20 percent that's protein, the 10 percent that's fat, the 5 percent that's mineral, and the 1 percent that's carbohydrate into our nearby plants and vegetation and trees.

Much of this we can't help. In short, we stink. Our bodies pollute not through any inherent toxicity, but through the simple virtue of our being human, of the airs we give off when our matter stops mattering.

We've long feared the idea that the dead might seep into the living. The ancient Romans banished their bodies outside their city walls; so did Napoleon. In the 1850s, London residents blamed cemeteries for a cholera outbreak and in Berlin, typhoid fever. A cemetery's gases tarnish silver, it's said, and, in warm summers, Parisians in Père-Lachaise and Montmartre will sample their arsenic-laced water and say it tastes slightly sweet, as if infected.

To counteract the body's pollutants, the World Health Organization recommends that cemetery keepers plant deep-rooted trees throughout their grounds. These soak up the body's byproducts and incorporate them into their vascular tissues. Their roots prevent the flow and seepage of contaminated groundwater. The trees are cheap and practical, "a natural filtration system," a wall that stands up long enough to be of some use.

Take the yew, for example, a tree so common in churchyard cemeteries it was known as "the tree of the dead." Robert Turner, the "strange, learned" seventeenth-century translator of mystical texts, praised it for drawing and imbibing "the gross and oleaginous Vapours exhaled out of the graves by the setting Sun." Monks believed the yew drove away devils, and Turner thought its roots must be poisonous because they "run and suck nourishment" from corpses, "the rankest poison that could be."

With this idea in mind, the Italian designers Anna Citelli and Raoul Bretzel have proposed a form of burial that will turn our bodies into trees. Their Capsula Mundi envisions placing bodies curled into the fetal position within biodegradable burial pods, which will then be interred directly beneath a tree or seed that grows upon the nutrients provided. Their design is just that, a design, but the inclination has stuck around for much longer. If you visit, for example, Brooklyn's Green-Wood Cemetery on a cold winter afternoon and see at the base of certain headstones a London planetree *In Loving Memory of Sergey Kats* or a Japanese cherry *In Honor of James J. Lian*, know that you are also looking, thermodynamically speaking, at Sergey Kats and James J. Lian themselves. We could say just a little more literally that we leave our bodies in trees, that if a tree becomes human in its splitting apart, then so too do humans become trees.

Since its founding in the 1830s, Green-Wood was renowned not just as a cemetery, but as one of New York City's finest arboretums—a home to 7,800 trees, a place where the air quality proved so rich that lichen carpeted the bark and the views so pleasing people picnicked there on weekends before the city outlawed it. In the early 1860s, only Niagara Falls drew more visitors per year. When Calvert Vaux and Frederick Law Olmsted planned their design for Central Park in the 1850s, they modeled it off Green-Wood.

The park I knew as a child then came from a city of the dead: the ginkgos whose leaves fell all at once, a superintendent's delight; the chestnut where my father buried the family hamster on his walk to work. And the American elm in the North Meadow that my mother memorialized my father within after he died, its ghost branches creeping over the chainlink of a baseball field where we used to play, the tree whose trunk I must have pissed on when I was drunk in high school and there was nowhere else to go. All those years I passed it without knowing what it would one day become.

When a tree is removed, my book on New York's trees tells me, there's "a hole in our understanding of the city." "Sometimes people love something to death," it says, describing why a particular tree is so well hid. "I'd like to rough that person up. It's a death sentence!" my mother adds when she hears of a tree on her block someone has cut into with a knife, deep enough that the xylem can no longer carry water up its trunk.

This makes sense, I think. I'd love them to death too— these mundane forms of resurrection we walk by every day.

∞

Another feng shui discussion my girlfriend and I have concerns the patchwork quilt. It sits folded on the red armchair that the cats like to scratch. My mother gave me this quilt for my birthday a few years ago. It is a mourning quilt, sewn together from scraps of my father's old clothes: a faded baby blue T-shirt with *Mr. Right* written across its chest; an old Mets shirt; the brim of a hat from Indian Lake, its stitched-on patch of Adirondacks and water. She has sewn likenesses of past family pets into the quilt—the yellow-gray cockatiel, an *E* for the dead dog.

For years, my mother did not know what to do with these old things. Now she has found a way—"Surprise! Happy birthday!"—for them to always stay with me. I am not to hang the quilt on the wall or use it as a decorative throw. My explicit instructions remain that I sleep underneath it. It's this that my girlfriend objects to: she does not want to use her boyfriend's dead father's clothes for warmth. And so the mourning quilt is relegated to the armchair, and I unfold it when I am cold and lying on the couch and reading about trees.

I have learned the hard way that when someone you love dies, the real shame of it is that your memory of them dies as well.

You end up with the silliest remnants. Like how my father, the Brazilian immigrant who spoke like the British if the British didn't try to speak like themselves, never fully learned prepositional nuance. How he often confused his instructions: "Get on the car," he'd say instead of "in." "Climb out" instead of "up." Or how the back half of "Adirondacks," in his mouth, became the frozen rum cocktail you sip with an umbrella and neon straw.

We can't really help forgetting, I don't think. I assign as much malice to it as I assign to the tree who steals another's sunlight. When it comes down to it, you do what you do to survive.

When the English sewed the earliest iterations of books from trees, they called these *codex*—a quire of pages stitched together, four parchment sheets folded to form eight leaves. They took the word from its Latin root, *caudex*: a block of wood or tree trunk.

After I move (new job, new town) and box up all my scattered books, my girlfriend buys me a broadside. I nail it to my wall. It's an excerpt from *About Trees*, a book in which the visual artist, Katie Holten, compiles various arboreal-themed texts using an invented tree typography. A is an apple; Q, a quaking aspen; E, an elm; C, a cedar; acorns as periods, and so on and so forth. Most of the trees, except for the conifers, lack leaves and so their bare forms on the page appear spectral, skeletal.

Holten's art collapses the difference between what something's made of and what something's made to mean. *About Trees*, Ida Bencke writes in her introduction, turns "language … back in on itself" when "matter and mattering are yet to be separated." It is "a memento of the arborescent nature of every book: that each piece of printed matter was once wood."

I would add to Bencke's claim, that if every piece of printed matter was once wood, then it was also once human.

∞

What I'm talking about is not so very difficult. Lye, sodium sulfate, what the Germans call the kraft process. An American elm in the North Meadow of Central Park. Cut through a branch or gather its leaves. Watch out for widow makers. Put the branch in a black garbage bag and carry it over one's shoulder the way one carries a body. If it's the right season, people would mistake it for a Christmas tree. Saw the wood, flake it, oatmeal it into pulp. Then a mother's casserole dish, a screen coaxed across a frame, a jar of soaked sodium hydroxide. Matter and mattering. Another way to break down wood. Repeat and repeat until noon or so and you hold these pages in your hands, your job of taking the broken and discarded and finding a new and useful arrangement.

These memories I have of my father, however silly, become precious. I grasp at anything that resists the word *disappear*, the word *gone*. Now his prepositions seem almost magical, as if his mistake could create a new reality. In the gap between the word he said and the word he meant, both somehow existed at once.

So that if I buried you under the right tree, eventually you would return. I would sit in the living room with my scattered books and I would hold you in my arms again. And even though you could not speak, I would read everything you had to tell me. I would underline, star, and scratch you up. You'd splay open while I ate my lunches, and I'd be careful not to spill coffee or ketchup, to crack your spine or dog-ear your corners too much. I would tell you I was sorry. Then I would fall asleep with my arms crossed over you on my chest and, for a while, I would not be so alone. I'd put you back on the bookshelf underneath your picture.

I know this would only be for a little while. Every resting place, especially this book of them, is half-lived. The pages are given up as soon as they are given over, fated to be remaindered and then recycled, a Mead journal or tax form, the glossy distended belly of a celebrity who has let himself go, the Tip #17 of 20 ways to please her between the sheets. Memory and body, already very small things, will be stripped and sinewed into pulp until someone else loses someone they love and puts pen to recycled paper and the old familiar story of metamorphosis begins again.

But in the meantime, in that pause between the word said and the word meant, wouldn't it feel like the gods? To reach out and feel bark where there once was skin. To find the love you failed returned a thousandfold. To brush against what is and is not true—a memory that calls out its disappearance, a being on its way to becoming something else. To realize I too have inherited these prepositions. We don't pass *away*, we pass *on*. We don't fade *away*, we fade *into*. That the simplest way I can put it will never make sense: you come back because you left, you go away because you were always here.

ACKNOWLEDGMENTS

Previous versions of these essays appeared in *Alaska Quarterly Review*, *CutBank*, *The Georgia Review*, *Kenyon Review Online*, *The Normal School*, and *Seneca Review*. Thank you to the editors of those journals. Particular thanks to Doug Carlson at *The Georgia Review* for shepherding "Overburden" through.

Thank you to Dan Smetanka for believing in this book and everyone at Counterpoint Press: Megan Fishmann, Jenny Alton, Shannon Price, Alisha Gorder.

Thank you, Matt McGowan.

My deep gratitude to the MFA program at the University of Arizona. In particular: Kate Bernheimer. Alison Deming. Ander Monson, the proverbial 3D-printed owl who watched over this all, dispensing and withholding wisdom. Manuel Muñoz, for being a close enough reader to point out this was Ander's role. The following friends and readers: Kati Standefer, Maya L. Kapoor, Lawrence

Lenhart, Nick Greer, Will Slattery, Ingrid Wenzler, Kirk Wisland, and many others.

Thank you to Jennifer Brice and Colgate University for giving me the time and opportunity to work on the book through the Olive B. O'Connor Fellowship. D. J. Thielke for the granola. Thank you as well to Bread Loaf Writers' Conference and the MacDowell Colony.

My aunts, Abigail and Eliza Thomas, have for years read whatever I've sent and responded with encouragement, even when undeserved. I wrote many of these essays with my grandfather Lewis Thomas (1913–1993) in mind.

I was once voted most likely to thank my cat in the Acknowledgments.

Thank you, Sarah Minor, for the tough and the love. Without you, this book wouldn't exist.

I wrote this in dedication to my mother, Judy Thomas, and father, Rafael Mira y Lopez (1947–2006).

ABOUT THE AUTHOR

THOMAS MIRA Y LOPEZ is from New York City. He earned an M.F.A. in creative nonfiction from the University of Arizona, and his work has appeared in *The Georgia Review*, *Kenyon Review Online*, and *The Normal School*, among other publications. He currently lives in North Carolina, where he is the 2017–2018 Kenan Visiting Writer at the University of North Carolina at Chapel Hill.